RUNAWAYS
AND
NON-RUNAWAYS
IN AN
AMERICAN SUBURB

RUNAWAYS AND NON-RUNAWAYS IN AN AMERICAN SUBURB

AN EXPLORATORY STUDY OF ADOLESCENT AND PARENTAL COPING

by
Albert R. Roberts
Associate Professor of Social Work
Seton Hall University

with
an Introduction by
Albert S. Allissi
University of Connecticut

Criminal Justice Center
Monograph Number 13

The John Jay Press
New York

Dedication

To my parents, Harry and Evelyn, whose love, devotion, and encouragement continue to serve as an inspiration to me.

To my wife, Beverly, whose love, tenderness, and intellectual stimulation continually enhance my appreciation of meaningful family interaction.

To all runaways and throwaways wherever they may be.

Acknowledgments

It is gratifying to acknowledge the individuals who made significant contributions to this study. I want to express my appreciation to Professors Joe Crymes, Paul Ephross, Don Fandetti, Joe Grau, and Agnes Hatfield for their scholarly comments and advice on an earlier draft of this study.

Several professionals were highly supportive in helping me gain access to the study sample. In particular, I would like to thank Nele Rand, Allen Layton, and Robert Manheimer for their encouragement and cooperation. Special thanks go to Harry Segessman for his constructive suggestions. To Beverly, my wife, I am indebted for her untiring efforts, emotional support, and grammatical assistance. The painstaking labor of typing several drafts of this manuscript was equaled only by Beverly's dependability throughout the long years of my doctoral studies.

Finally, I thank all of the youths who shared with me their feelings, stresses, and fears. Without the willingness of these youths to reveal their inner turmoil this research would not have been possible.

Table
of
Contents

Introduction

Every year an estimated million people run away from home while another million leave their homes and families by mutual consent or as "throwaways." The seriousness of the problem is made clear enough by the stark reality of the vicitimization, street lives in drugs and sex, and mass torture murders that have shocked us in recent years. But beyond this the sheer magnitude of human suffering and anxiety created by this runaway problem in the lives of millions of children and their families is difficult to calculate and comprehend. For a nation committed to improving the life of all its people, the vast storehouse of hopelessness, frustration, and broken dreams cannot be ignored or accepted as a necessary product of stressful parent-child relationships that none can do anything about.

The helping professions cannot be satisfied with limited after-the-fact interventions such as hot lines, temporary shelters, and group homes for runaways. Until we know much more about how the runaway phenomena is fostered and nurtured in the life experiences of young people, there is little we will be able to do to get at the basic causes. What do we know about the kind of stressful events, interpersonal traumas, varying successful as well as unsuccessful coping mechanisms associated with choosing the runaway alternative?

Such are the questions addressed in Dr. Roberts' study. His is not just another comparison control group study designed to scientifically demonstrate the existence of specific identifiable variables found to be associated with runaway behavior. The scope of attention is not narrowed to individual "attributes" or even "factors" affecting such behavior. More significantly, he sheds light on concrete episodes, crucial situational and interactional variables. Parents and others so essential to the process are brought into the study process not only as a reliability check but much more importantly as a significant component in the interactional drama that brings about runaway behavior.

Dr. Roberts presents his case in a clear and convincing manner. Practitioners will find his scholarly approach to the problem refreshingly concrete and practical. The rich descriptions of crisis events, the construction of analytical typologies of runaway behavior, and the poignant comparisons of runaway and conventional responses of youths to adjustment problems contribute significantly to our knowledge base. The research method utilized is particularly instructive for those of us who are interested in advancing qualitative research methodologies in social work. Finally, studies such as this can do much to influence social policy decisions in the juvenile justice system where the need for sound and insightful data is so important.

I would like to highlight, using a broader perspective, what I see to be significant about this work for the social work profession and juvenile field of justice.

A wise social work educator of mine often told her students, whenever they were unable to resolve field problems in spite of persistent hard work, to stop and take a look at the underlying assumptions and definitions they were taking for granted in their approach. Although we certainly hesitate to admit it, we seldom see things the way they really are. We see only certain aspects — those that we have been taught to abstract using the currency of our own cultural symbols. As Walter Lippman said in his famous aphorism, "We do not first see, then define, we define first and then we see. . ." Clearly, what we perceive or overlook depends largely on ready-made concepts and definitions that we take for granted. It is a curious fact that we have in our language words or labels for "runaways," "truants," and "status offenders," and so on while we have few terms for parents, teachers and others who may be instrumental in surfacing this kind of behavior in their charges? Worst still we have only a few workable concepts that get at the interactional process itself — a process which studies continue to document as crucial in perpetuating the runaway problem.

As a social work educator, my objective for some years now has been to encourage students to expand the repertoire of concepts and to develop a range of perspectives from which they could "tailormake" concepts which will be of value in their practice. The essence of the social work enterprise, to me, stems from the social worker's concern over the social functioning of people. Hence, the client, patient, group, or family member can never be divorced conceptually from his or her network of interpersonal relationships for separate intervention. Clearly, the social interaction in which the individual functions serves as the context in which service has to be given. And those concepts that focus on interpersonal interaction, systemic relationships and related social cultural and "situational" determinants of behavior are essential parts of the social worker's repertoire.

Frustration and disappointment are not strangers to social workers and others in the helping professions who seek to find practical ways to help people modify their interpersonal relationships. However tempted we may have been in the past to define social-emotional problems from the standpoint of the individualized client, insurmountable forces were always working beyond the individual that we could not ignore in spite of our inability to address them effectively. For the most part, however, our programs continue to separate the individual from his or her social context to be isolated as a source of concern and target for change. Although the focus on the interactional unit is essential, we still sorely lack the technology that will help us to address the international dilemmas within the context of societal norms and traditions.

Dr. Roberts' study is significant in that it forces us to recognize that the problem behavior of our youths such as seen in the runaway in itself lacks meaning unless it is seen in the situational and interaction context in which it is fostered and subject to social and legal controls. The focus on episodes, on levels of parent-youth conflict and differing social/cultural determinants not only contributes to our growing knowledge of interactional phenomena but more importantly provides us with some concrete materials upon which we can begin to intervene where it matters most.

In this regard, many of the findings here are followed up with a variety or relevant recommendations which are important to social workers. The dilemma, however, is real: how can we develop suitable programs that focus on the interactional networks, and situational contexts in which problems emerge — given the state of our current practice, knowledge and skills? This is a complex area. And it is not altogether clear just how much of our efforts to increase parent effectiveness, enhance parent-child relationships, develop networking group and family interventions will successfuly affect the sources of the runaway problem. Dr. Roberts provides us with some valuable clues here and goes further to identify many areas, where the potential for further research seems promising.

The research method utilized here represents still another major contribution to the social work profession. For many years now, social workers have been somewhat uneasy with the role of research in their work. To be sure, social work researchers do contribute to our knowledge base, to building theory and to guiding and developing practice. Similarly, practitioners regularly utilize research findings to assess needs, evaluate program effectiveness, influence decision-makers, and determine policies and so on. But the recognized difficulties in researching variables which are somewhat abstract and yet so critical to practice continues to generate the feeling that the research method itself needs to be much more responsive to social work concerns. Dr. Roberts' "qualitative" orientation is a good example of what's needed. His use of many rich descriptions of the processes influencing behavior is essential to a proper understanding of the variables. Such efforts to utilize verbatum data to get directly at the quality of the phenomena under study is particularly important in exploratory studies and adds much to our appreciation of what is really going on.

The findings, of course, have many implications for formulating policy and influencing legislation in the child welfare and juvenile justice fields. The failure of governmental authorities to deal adequately with the full range of child welfare concerns and the limited involvement and accountablity of the private agencies in dealing with runaways has resulted in a larger voice by police, courts, and correctional authorities in handling juveniles in "trouble." There is, however, a serious debate going on across the country whether the so-called status offender should continue to be defined as a law-violator subjected to the jurisdiction of the juvenile courts. Only a few would continue to look to the courts to achieve the "rehabilitative ideal" which seemed so promising in the juvenile court movement. The perspective is equally narrow for those who would define the runaway behavior in terms of emotional disturbances. Yet, we continue to rely on such jural and medical solutions as the individual runaway is continually placed in the proverbial "fishbowl" for analysis and proper "disposition."

However, one chooses to interpret the findings reported here, it is patently clear that runaway behavior is anything but an isolated law-violating or psychogenic happening. Indeed, were we to re-examine those concepts we take for granted, it would be clear that the role of parents and other individuals affecting runaway behavior contributes as much to the problem as does the so-called runaway.

The challenge to social policy makers in the juvenile justice field is clear enough. How can we reach the runaway in any meaningful way and at the same time reach those who are instrumental in precipitating runaway behavior? The data here makes it clear that runaway behavior represents a natural outcome of unsuccessful interpersonal encounters. This must be explored to the utmost, and policies need to be developed that takes this into account. It will become increasingly difficult to carry out "business as usual" in the face of such insights.

— Albert S. Alissi, D.S.W.
Professor of Social Work
University of Connecticut

RUNAWAYS
AND
NON-RUNAWAYS
IN AN
AMERICAN SUBURB

I. The Runaway Phenomenon

She told me to get out. Yelling and throwing things at me. She kept saying, "You killed your father." I ran to my friend. They let me stay. I hid in the basement.

— a sixteen year old runaway boy.

I was throwing up all day and went to the school nurse. She told me I had a concussion. The nurse touched my nose and it hurt. She felt it and said it was cracked. She asked what happened. I told her I had a fight with some girl. She kept asking me questions and she said for a very young girl she hit pretty hard. Finally I broke down and told her it was my father. She wanted to call the office for someone for child abuse. I wouldn't let her. My father would kill me if I reported him. I was dizzy and I couldn't see straight. I was off balance. She sent me home and called my father and told him to call the hospital.

— a fifteen year old runaway girl.

Official estimates of the number of runaways in the United States are staggering; each year hundreds of thousands of minors between the ages of twelve and eighteen run away from their homes. Several estimates indicate that well over a million youths leave their homes annually.

Runaways are often frightened, hungry, and lonely. Often they leave home without enough money to pay for basic necessities of life like food and shelter. Sometimes plans to runaway have been made ahead of time, and alternative living arrangements have been made. However, in most cases, running away seems to take place from a spur-of-the-moment impulse. As a result, some youths find themselves sleeping in parked cars, under the bleachers at a nearby high school, in a friend's basement or backyard, and even in a four foot by six foot Salvation Army clothing container. Intense hunger and malnutrition are not uncommon. In order to survive, some runaways borrow money from friends or relatives. Those without relatives or close friends may end up "hustling" by selling drugs, shoplifting, panhandling, prostituting themselves, or exchanging sexual favors for food and a place to spend the night. Especially in large cities, many runaways become victims who are assaulted, coerced into prostitution, raped, and even murdered.

The runaway phenomenon can be viewed as a social problem, because it affects a large number of people in society, is a violation of societal norms, and is viewed as a condition that is capable of improvement through social intervention (Shellow, et. al., 1967:1; for a sociological definition of social problems, see: Johnson, 1973, Chapter 1; Poplin, 1978, Chapter 1; and Henry, 1978: 1-3).

According to recent statistics, the number of youths who leave their homes is increasing. Opinion Research Corporation's (November, 1976) national survey on the prevalence of adolescent runaways indicated that each year, 733,000 youths between the ages of ten and seventeen years of age leave their homes without permission. Nationally, the prevalence of runaways was documented by Senator Birch Bayh (1974) in testimony before the House of Representatives' Subcommittee on Equal Opportunities of the Committee on Education and

Labor:

> . . .the estimated one million youngsters who annually run
> away from home. Runaways pose a problem of growing pro-
> portions as more and more younger and younger children,
> primarily girls, take to the streets. The FBI reports that in
> 1972, 199,185 youths were arrested as runaways. This is an
> increase of 39 percent between 1967 and 1972. More
> significantly, the most common age arrested was in the 13 to
> 14 age bracket (p. 159.).

Many runaways are not included in official tabulations because
of underreporting due to parental neglect, embarrassment, and
apathy, and an estimate of one million may well be low. As
Shellow, et. al. (1967) stated:

> We knew that those [runaways] who were reported missing to
> the police were merely the tip of the runaway iceberg and that
> beneath the surface lay an undetermined number invisible to
> public agencies.

The dangers of the runaway problem were gruesomely and
emphatically brought to the attention of the entire nation by
the mass murders in Houston which were uncovered in August,
1973 (New York *Times,* August 14, 1973, p.1). That many of the
twenty-seven tortured teeenagers were found to have been
runaways (New York *Times,* August 14, 1973, p. 18, and
August 16, 1973, p. 17) led the Houston Police Department to
issue publicly their estimate that over 5,000 youths run away
from their homes in the Houston area each year (New York
Times, August 11, 1973, p. 17). Police in Chicago reported
handling 16,500 runaways in 1972 (*Times,* August 27, 1973, p.
57) and the New York City Police Department estimates that
there are over 20,000 runaways under sixteen years of age in the
city at any given time (Sheppard, August 16, 1973:17; and Ritter, 1979:24).

The runaway phenomenon is not limited to the inner city of
large metropolitan areas. Youths from suburban middle class
families are also running away in large numbers. Long Island
authorities estimate that 10,000 youths run away from home in
Nassau and Suffolk Counties each year (Neugebauer, 1979, sec-

tion II:1). Runaway statistics from the Washington, D.C. suburbs indicate that affluent Montgomery County, Maryland has 1,800 runaways per year and Fairfax County, Virginia has over 1,300 runaways per year (Mullins, 1979). The latter figures do not include those cases which never get reported to the police; underreporting may be especially high in middle and upper class suburban families.

SOCIETAL RESPONSES TO RUNAWAYS

Runaways began receiving national media and press coverage in the late 1960's when thousands of middle class youths, many of whom were college-age, left their homes to adopt the hippie life-style. Two locations seem to have attracted most of the publicity as meccas for the runaways: Haight-Ashbury near San Francisco and the East Village in New York City. A decade later, the types of youth who run away and the conditions surrounding their actions have changed. The hippie movement which advocated a group camaraderie, communal living, peace and love is no more. During the 1970's, youths are reported to be leaving home at younger and younger ages; twelve, thirteen, and fourteen year-old runaways are not uncommon.

The public has become aware of the extent and nature of child abuse recently, and researchers have been exploring the many ramifications of such abuse. One ramification may be the intense desire of youths in early adolescence to flee from abuse in a home, even when an alternate living situation has not been secured.

The public has also become aware of the vulnerability of young runaways, particularly in densely populated cities. The youths are coaxed and lured into prostitution and then forced to continue prostitution through threats of and actual demonstrations of physical violence.

This increased awareness of child abuse and runaways on the part of the general public and federal legislators is demonstrated by the development of two toll-free nationwide hotlines; the passage of the Runaway Youth Act; and the establishment of runaway shelters nationwide, largely with federal funds.

Runaway Hotline formerly known as Operation Peace of Mind (POM) is a twenty-four hour a day line (800-231-6946) which was established in the aftermath of the brutal murders of twenty-seven boys in August, 1973. The hotline was established due to the anguish and suffering of parents who, having heard about the Houston murders, were anxious about the welfare and safety of their runaway children. The discovery of the boys' mutilated bodies led to a flood of calls to the Houston police from parents throughout the United States and especially from those living in Texas. A New York *Times* inquiry revealed a similar torrent of calls from hundreds of concerned parents of missing youths to police in other cities as well (Weisman, 1973:8).

The national hotline located in Texas was established through a combined effort of donations and volunteer staff. Approximately a month after the Houston bodies had been uncovered, the Runaway Hotline began receiving calls on September 11, 1973 (Hevener, 1975:1). Eight months later, federal funding was obtained to maintain the toll-free hotline. The hotline is currently funded by Texas' Governor's Office for Volunteer Services.

Another twenty-four hour a day, toll-free nationwide hotline (800-621-4000) for runaways is the National Runaway Switchboard in Chicago. It had established a local hotline in August, 1974 as the result of a federal grant. The general purposes of both of these hotlines are to relay confidential messages from youths to their parents and to provide referrals to community resources like emergency shelters, counseling centers, medical clinics, and legal aid agencies.

Runaways learn about the existence of these hotlines through television, radio, and word-of-mouth. An example of the effectiveness of television in alerting youths to these hotlines is a TV documentary on runaways which was aired on May 29, 1980. The Runaway Hotline in Texas reported a sharp increase in calls during the three day period following the telecast.

> The recent television documentary entitled Runaways is a perfect example of how much publicity affects our program . . . On Thursday, May 29, the Hotline received over

500 calls; on Friday, May 30, over 300 calls; and on Saturday,
May 31, over 280 calls. A normal day usually means around
120 calls in a 24-hour period (Woodward, 1980).

The passage of Title III of the Juvenile Justice and Delinquency Prevention Act of 1974, called the Runaway Youth Act,
made available millions of dollars in federal funds for the
establishment of runaway shelters and counseling services
(Public Law 93-415, 1974). The bill to provide needed services
for runaways was first proposed in Congress in 1971 but the initial legislation did not pass. The findings as stated in the Act
are as follows:

(1) the number of juveniles who leave and remain away from
home without parental permission has increased to alarming
proportions, creating a substantial law enforcement problem
for the communities inundated, and significantly en-
dangering the young people who are without resources and
live on the street;
(2) the exact nature of the problem is not well defined because
national statistics on the size and profile of the runaway
youth population are not tabulated;
(3) many such young people, because of their age and situation, are urgently in need of temporary shelter and counseling services;
(4) the problem of locating, detaining, and returning runaway
children should not be the responsibility of already over-
burdened police departments and juvenile justice authorities;
and
(5) in view of the interstate nature of the problem, it is the
responsibility of the Federal Government to develop accurate
reporting of the problem nationally and to develop an effective system of temporary care outside the law enforcement
structure (pp. 20-21).

As a direct result of the passage of the Runaway Youth Act,
federal funds were used to develop runaway programs across
the country. They provide emergency services like food, shelter,
and counseling services in a safe and wholesome environment
which is separate from law enforcement and juvenile justice

systems. Sixty-six grants were awarded in 1975 during the first funding cycle to support programs in thirty-two states, Puerto Rico, Guam, and the District of Columbia. To be eligible to receive federal funds, the Act mandates that runaway houses: 1. be situated in a location which is easily accessible to runaway youths; 2. "have a maximum capacity of no more than twenty children;" 3. make adequate plans for contacting the families of youths, if state law requires that action; "assur[e] the safe return of the child according to the best interest of the child;" and "provid[e] for other appropriate alternative living arrangements." Federal funds continue to be provided for the development of new services and the expansion and upgrading of existing services for runaways.

Problems still remain. Many runaway youths never benefit from the services of these federal programs because young people are not aware of the existence of the runaway shelters or no shelter is located in their vicinity. Often youths are eager to begin living on their own and do not realize the difficulties they may encounter, especially when they do not have enough money.

Law enforcement officials are alert for minors who run away from home. Their treatment of youthful suspects depends to a great extent upon the nature of the officer who finds them and a state's laws pertaining to status offense. The type of legal treatment given to a runaway may entail kindly and thoughtful crisis intervention like release to the youth's parents or referral to a runaway shelter, or it may result in harsh reprimands, antagonism, adjudication as a juvenile delinquent, and possibly imprisonment.

Teenagers who are on their own with no place to go are vulnerable targets for victimizers like con men, drug dealers, and pimps. Thousands of young runaway girls have voluntarily become or are coerced into becoming prostitutes by pimps in large cities like Boston, Minneapolis, New Orleans and New York. All too often these girls, who are usually between twelve and sixteen years of age, are raped and beaten if they refuse to comply. Others are lured by promises that they can get rich quickly, while also acquiring the affection and "protection" of their newly found pimp (Raab, Oct. 30, 1977: pp. 1 & 21 and

Raab, Nov. 2, 1977, p. B3). Teenage runaway boys seem to be no less vulnerable than are the girls to prostitution, either under the supervision of a pimp or on their own as a quick way to earn money to survive on the streets. Those boys who turn to homosexual prostitution have been labeled as "chicken hawks" by the news media (Vecsey, 1976:37). Police have given accounts of the brutal conditions these runaway boys and girls have endured. One police officer reported on a sixteen year-old girl who had been recruited in Minneapolis when she was only fourteen. The girl stated that she had given her pimp more than $100,000 during the eighteen months she had been working the streets. Her pimp had given her a quota — to earn at least $150 a night, six nights a week. When another girl told her pimp that she wanted to return to her parents, he broke her jaw and forced her in that condition to continue working the streets (Raab, Oct. 30, 1977:21).

THE RUNAWAYS AND NON-RUNAWAYS

In addition to the adjustment to adolescence with which all youths are confronted, the teenagers in this study have been victims of ongoing verbal and/or physical abuse. Unlike youths who flee to Florida or California for a brief time in a warmer climate or those who suddenly stay overnight at a friend's house to manipulate their parents, many of the runaways in this study ran from conflict-ridden homes where physical and verbal abuse reoccurred.

Sixty individuals, thirty of whom were runaway adolescents and thirty of whom formed a comparison group of non-runaway adolescents were interviewed at "Runaway Retreat," a pseudonym for a suburban counseling center. All of them were under eighteen years of age and had stayed away from their homes without parental permission for at least twenty-four hours. The non-runaway group was randomly selected from "Suburban High," another pseudonym. To provide for verification of the responses of the runaways and non-runaways, ten parents of the runaways and twelve parents of the non-runaways were interviewed.

There are two distinct yet related purposes of the research in this exploratory study. An attempt is made to determine to what extent do runaways experience stressful events before leaving their homes and to gather open-ended interview data from runaways and non-runaways to determine if any patterns emerge which suggest that differing stresses and coping mechanisms have been used by youths who run away from home in comparison to those who do not run away.

RATIONALE FOR THE STUDY

For some individuals, adolescence is a time when critical demands are made on them to deal with major stressful events like a parent's death, divorce, physical abuse, alcoholism, severe illness, or hospitalization. A significant hazard is posed by these events when they affect adolescents who, developmentally, are already in a period of conflict and transition.

Caplan (1964), Jacobson, et. al. (1965), Aguilera, et. al. (1970), and Parad (1971) have described the situational crises which arise from stressful events like the death of a loved one. In crisis theory, the major emphasis is not upon the stressful event itself but upon the individual's reaction to the stress. A crisis state is defined as a significant disruption in an individual characterized by feelings of helplessness and confusion and an inability to reduce tension and solve one's problem by previously learned modes of coping.

Crisis theorists have also described another category of crisis — maturational crisis — as part of the normal processes of human growth and development. Maturational crisis evolves over a period of several years and usually results in changes in one's physical appearance and character. Adolescence is often viewed as a maturational crisis stage significant to the formation of one's unique identity and a positive self-image (Erikson, 1950, 1956). Adolescence has been acknowledged as a period of socialization in which an individual is characteristically faced with social and moral dilemmas regarding a desire for growing autonomy, goal setting for the future, and pressure from peer groups to experiment with drugs and to engage in sexual behavior.

The individuals in this study were in the middle of two major types of crises — maturational and situational, and although the maturational development of these adolescents was not assessed, an effort was made to determine the extent to which adolescent runaways were in situational crises.

II. Research Perspectives on Runaways

The primary emphasis of most of the studies and research on adolescent runaways is an attempt to unravel the sometimes diverse motives for and causes of runaway episodes. However, little material exists on the specific topic of suburban runaways and on the extent to which stressful events and accompanying crisis seem to predispose adolescents to run away from home.

A literature review uncovered serious weaknesses in past studies taken as a whole: there is no common language; use of concepts varies greatly; and different approaches are used because researchers identify themselves with different disciplines like social work, criminology, psychology, psychiatry, or sociology. Because of the complexity of the runaway problem and the lack of a unifying conceptual framework, integration of the literature becomes extremely difficult.

However, three fundamental perspectives on adolescent runaways dominate the literature: psychopathological theories, situational theories, and typologies of runaways.

PSYCHOPATHOLOGICAL INTERPRETATIONS

The studies which approach runaways psychopathologically view a runaway individual as suffering from some form of personal disturbance like poor impulse control, neurosis, unresolved Oedipal conflicts, severe narcissistic disorders or a low self-concept.

Several researchers during the 1930's and 1940's postulated that running away is a reaction to the youth's individual psychopathology. Armstrong (1937) viewed the typical runaway as a psychoneurotic from a low-income minority group, who was mentally deficient and who experienced a great deal of fear, distress, and insecurity. Riemer (1940) stressed that running away reflects an "extremely negative character," and "constitutes a severe narcissistic disorder."

Investigators studying adolescent runaways within the juvenile justice system seem to have consistently focused on the youths' delinquent and psychologically disturbed behavior (Armstrong, 1937; Leventhal, 1964; Riemer, 1940; Robey, et. al., 1964; and Rosenheim, 1940).

Robey and his associates (1964) took a psychoanalytic view in their study of forty-two middle class runaway girls who had been referred to the Framingham (Massachusetts) Court Clinic. Focusing on family pathology, they attributed runaway behavior to a strong Oedipal influence and the threat of an incestuous relationship, resulting from "a disturbed marital relationship, inadequate control by the parents over their own and the girls' impulses, deprivation of love of the mother" and pressure upon the daughter to assume the maternal role. Due to the lack of maternal warmth and affection, girls become hypermature while maintaining a goal of oral gratification to compensate for the lack of maternal affection. Robey, et. al. maintained that the girls' runaway acts can be viewed as an adaptive response against being forced into the mother's role; without treatment, the girls' futures were not promising.

Leventhal (1963) concluded from his study of sixteen runaways that a lack of generalized control over factors like unbearable home situations led to runaway behavior. The runaways perceived themselves to be in situations in which they were humiliated, nagged, and constantly on their guard against threats to their egos. To Leventhal it seemed reasonable that individuals, finding themselves in situations that pressured and humiliated them and over which they felt that they had no control, would remove themselves from those situations.

Research studies based on data from agencies other than the juvenile courts also reported poor impulse control, depression and low self-esteem among runaways (Joos, Debuyst, and Sepulchre-Cassiers, 1970; Robins and O'Neal, 1959).

SITUATIONAL INTERPRETATIONS

While not denying the possible significance of individual psychopathology, several studies have viewed youths' leaving home as a result of situational problems. The arena for these problems is frequently the family, although some findings indicate that these problems originate in school, peer pressure, and the interaction among family, school, and peer pressure.

Shellow and his associates (1967) viewed runaways as falling into two groups — the psychopathological group and the situational group. However, the primary focus of their analysis emphasizes the importance of the environmental and situational circumstances of the runaways they studied. Shellow contends that "runaways show serious personal disturbance" as a result of their individual psychopathology and interprets running away as "an adaptive response to situational pressures, the origins of which may lie in ordinary family conflicts or even in general economic conditions" (p. 1).

Shellow's view of running away as an adaptive response is consistent with that of Outland (1938), Balser (1939), Lowery (1941), and Goldmeier and Dean (1973). Outland (1938) concluded that running away was a response to economic hardship and a quest for adventure. Balser found that first-time runaways solved their problems by the runaway episode. Lowery (1941) concluded that running away seemed to be a healthy mode of response to an intolerable situation. Goldmeier and Dean (1973) viewed running away as a response to the problems like poor grades in school and difficulties approaching teachers and parents that youths encounter prior to running. Shellow, et. al.'s study was based on a sample of 731 runaways, ten to seventeen years of age from Prince Georges County, Maryland. Data were obtained from police records and interviews with runaways and their parents. The sample was characterized by: conflict at home over rules and school performance; broken homes (forty-eight percent); considerable difficulty with academic subjects and many school absences; little history of other delinquency; and minimal involvement or accompanying satisfaction in part-time jobs and after-school clubs. Two groups of runaways were found: a small group who had significant individual or family pathology and the majority who were not seriously disturbed. To youths in the latter group, leaving home was a way of dealing with momentary dissatisfaction at home, at school, or with peers.

Shellow and his associates concluded that there was little seasonal variation in the number of runaway episodes; boys ran each day of the week, while girls ran more frequently on Friday and Saturday than any other days of the week; girls were more likely to leave between 6:00 P.M. and midnight while boys were more likely to leave during the daylight hours; in most cases, (fifty-one percent) the runaway youth was the oldest child in his or her home; only fifty-two percent of the juveniles lived with both of their natural parents; two thirds of the parents of runaways indicated that their child's school performance was a problem; one-time runaways were likely to return on their own and to be away less than two days (only twenty-eight percent were away from home more than two days); repeaters frequently tended to be away longer than two days (forty-two percent were away longer than two days).

Based on questionnaires which Shellow's staff administered to 1,350 students in eleven schools, it was estimated that only one of every six runaways is reported in the police records. It was also revealed that one-third of the students who had not run away had seriously considered doing so.

D'Angelo's (1974) sample of eighty-two runaways was obtained from four agencies (Juvenile Diagnostic Center, Juvenile Detention Home, Huckleberry House, and Buckeye Boys Ranch) and his sample of eighty-two non-runaways (thirty-nine percent) was obtained from six high schools in Franklin County, Ohio. His study reported that more runaways (thirty-nine percent) came from broken homes than non-runaways (twenty-two percent). When asked to report how well their parents got along in comparison to their friends' parents, twenty-five percent of the runaways indicated that "their parents got along worse than other parents compared to only nine percent for the controls."

In order to learn about the strength of the relationship between parents, the runaways and non-runaways were asked how often their parents argued in comparison to their friends' parents: ". . . thirty-four percent of the runaways reported their parents argued more than other parents compared to only thirteen percent for the controls." To determine whether runaways sought the help of "one or both" parents in handling a problem, the respondents were asked to name "the three most likely persons [they] would be willing to seek help from if [they] were to get into trouble." Forty-nine percent of the runaways listed parents in comparison to eighty two percent of the non-runaways. The majority or forty-five of the eighty-four runaways reported that problems with parents were their reason for running away. Other reasons were related to parental pressures, such as "feel unloved" (six runaways), and "anxiety and insecurity" (four runaways). Over one-third or thirty-four runaways did not report specific destinations, but most of them or twenty-five youths who did report a destination said they were headed out-of-state. In almost "every instance, these destinations were never reached." Respondents were asked to check-off one of five possible categories which approximated their academic standing among their school peers. Only thirty-eight percent of the runaways, in contrast to twenty-eight percent of the non-runaways checked "below average" as their class standing. Although D'Angelo's study was thorough, it is limited by the inherent methodological bias of having each youth complete a questionnaire consisting mostly of structured questions accompanied by a list of several possible answers.

TYPOLOGIES OF RUNAWAYS

Several schemas for classifying runaways have been reported

in the literature (Dunford and Brennan, 1976; English, 1973; Greene and Esselstyn, 1972; and Homer, 1973). These descriptions of "ideal types" of runaways often appear to be basically similar, focusing on the youths' reasons for running.

Three types of runaways are consistently described as those who run from an "intolerable family situation," those seeking adventure" or those with "school problems." The authors of these recent articles each appear to be applying different labels to the same types of runaway behaviors; adolescents who have run away because of family conflicts have been referred to as the "running from" category by Homer (1973), sometimes as "runaways" by English (1973), and as the anxious runaway by Greene and Esselstyn (1972).

Greene and Esselstyn's "rootless runaway" girl was an adventurer, for she is defined as a pleasure-seeker requiring immediate gratification. Similarly, Homer's (1973) runaway girls, classified in the "running to" group, were seeking excitement and adventure through a variety of experiences forbidden at home.

English's (1973) four-tiered system for classifying runaways consists of the "floaters," "runaways," "splitters," and "hard road freaks." He defines the "floaters" as those youths who fantasize about leaving home; if they actually do run away, they return within forty-eight hours. In order to relieve built-up tensions, floaters test the idea of running by talking about it and then usually change their mind. "Runaways" included those youths who were leaving a destructive family situation, those who ran with the hope of calling attention to a situation and thereby obtaining help, and those who ran from the fear of, or actual discovery of, a personal secret or an unshareable problem like an unwed pregnancy. "Splitters" were youths who ran because of minor frustrations. Part of the splitter's motivation derived from their peers' positive image of those who ran away. "Hard road freaks" or street people generally were older runaways between the ages of seventeen and twenty who had severed ties with their homes and lived a nomadic life style.

Greene and Esselstyn (1972:16-18), in their discussion of ungovernable and incorrigible girls, describe three distinct types of runaway girls — the rootless, the anxious, and the terrified.

A "rootless runaway" is a pleasure-seeker who often required immediate gratification. She is likely to drop out of school, quit a series of jobs, use drugs, and become sexually active. Although she was probably lavished with praise as a child, her parents never set limits for her. During adolescence, she has frequent periods of depression, which frightens her family. They "for the first time set limits on her. The girl rebels, runs away, and is soon taken into custody." After the family comes to her aid, the girl returns home and has her way with everything until a curfew or rule is imposed. Then the girl protests, rebels, and runs again.

An "anxious runaway" frequently is from a multi-problem family. She often has to help with household chores, rearing younger siblings, and worrying about finances. If her father is living at home, she may experience his physical and verbal abuse resulting from his excessive drinking. The anxious youth flees for a few hours or overnight to seek help for herself or for her family. She wants to talk to someone, often to a friend's mother. She is glad to return home.

A "terrified runaway" flees from her father's or step-father's sexual advances. When incest does take place, the mother may be aware and subtly encourage it because "it displaces the husband's sexual demands from herself to her daughter." The mother may feel that marriage and children have prevented her from realizing her potential. A terrified runaway often invites many of her friends to visit her home, but stays away from the house as often as she can to avoid being alone with her sexually abusive male relation. The girl often runs in terror to escape sexual abuse, and her sense of guilt is great, because she views herself as the agent of inevitable family collapse.

Homer (1973) studied twenty runaway girls who were between the ages of thirteen and sixteen. His study delineated two distinct types of runaways: those girls who were running away from family problems and those who seemed to be pleasure-seekers, running to places or people who provided them with sex, drugs, liquor or truancy. Within the "running from" category, six of the seven girls indicated that they could not tolerate their home situations or one or both parents. In the "running to" group, ten of the thirteen girls indicated that they enjoyed running away and liked the friends they met on the run. Only two of the ten girls said that their mothers did not understand them. Homer found that the previously mentioned six out of seven girls in the "running from" category appeared to benefit from individual and family therapy and stopped running. In contrast, nine of the thirteen girls categorized in the "running to" group, continued having frequent runaway episodes and "usually did not return until they were picked up by the police" (Homer, 1973:478).

A four-level typology developed by Dunford and Brennan (1976) is based on a classification resulting from runaways' scores on different standardized scales. In addition to studying the parental relationships of runaways, these researchers investigated the youths' grades in school, their level of self-esteem, and their involvement in delinquency and drug use. In the Dunford and Brennan taxonomy, youths are classified into four types. Type 1 is comprised solely of self-confident and unrestrained runaway girls. Having poor parental relations, they feel ineffective at influencing the decisions their parents make about the girl's life. Parental control is characterized by little discipline and much unsupervised freedom. These girls had high grades, high self-esteem scores, and positive attitudes toward peers and teachers. Type 2 is comprised of well-adjusted runaway youths, characterized by positive parental relationships. They do not perceive their parents as employing excessive control or punishment as a means of discipline. They feel good about school and their self-esteem scores are high. These youths are most likely to run away from their homes for adventure and to prove to themselves that they can get to a distant place on their own. Type 3 is represented by youths who are very involved with delinquency, characterized by poor relationships with parents and failing at school. They have a mean grade point average of "D+ ", a high level of parental rejection, parental marital conflict, involvement in delinquent activities, and drug use. These youths registered the highest scores for expressed parental rejection, as well as for perceived rejection implicitly due to few parental demands for achievement made upon them and few rewards offered. Type 4 is comprised of fleeing youth. These youths' parents "exercise excessive control and make exceedingly high achievement demands." The parents display little desire to help or talk over their children's problems. These runaways perceive a high level of parental rejection, have low self-esteem scores, and score high on being deprived of privileges.

Shellow, et. al (1967) have aptly summarized the whole issue concerning why children run away from home.

Research on children who ran away from home has a history of some forty years or more. This past research does not present a single sharp image of the runaway child but rather a blurred and shifting configuration. Why children run away from home and the meaning of running away to the child, to his family, and to society seem not to be constants but everchanging functions of time and place (p. 28).

III. Research Design

SITE

The data for this study were collected in interviews with thirty runaways who had come to a private youth counseling agency, and thirty non-runaways who were enrolled at a nearby high school. To insure confidentiality of youths, both the agency and the school requested that the study not identify them; consequently, they have been designated as "Runaway Retreat" and "Suburban High." Runaway Retreat is located in the southeastern part of New York State on the north shore of Long Island. It serves youths from a highly populated suburban county with a population of over one million people. Most of the youths served by the agency reside in the two townships adjacent to their facilities. Most of the youths who are counselled by Runaway Retreat's staff are between the ages of thirteen and seventeen. Runaway Retreat operates two facilities within close proximity of each other. One is a drop-in center which provides individual, group and parent counseling, and family therapy. The second facility is a home having a capacity of eight. There, up to six weeks of shelter and group counseling for youths is provided. Most youths have histories of family conflict, drug use, or runaway behavior. They are placed in the group home temporarily while they await placement in a foster home, long-term residential facility, modified independent living situation (for example, as a mother's helper, they receive room and board in exchange for doing baby sitting and some kitchen chores), or return home.

SAMPLE

The datum was gathered from in-depth interviews with thirty runaways who were seen by Runaway Retreat's staff between June 14 and August 30, 1977. All of these youths were under eighteen years of age and had left their homes without permission for more than twenty-four hours. They were introduced either by their intake counselor or by one of the youths who frequented the "rap room" at Runaway Retreat's Drop-in Center. A total of thirty-three youths were referred, and only three of them refused to be interviewed. Since the researcher participated in the agency's group counseling sessions during most of one summer, the adolescents related to him as an extra counselor.

The means of validating the information provided by the runaways was to interview as many of their parents or guardians as possible. Ten parents of the runaways were interviewed. Most of the runaways' parents were reluctant to be interviewed, although the researcher expressed a willingness to interview them at their convenience, day or evening.

A basic weakness of research on crises, particularly research on runaways in crisis, is that usually no attempt has been made to compare clinic samples of runaways who may be in crisis with any comparative group of "normal" adolescents. Therefore, a comparison sample was also interviewed. The interviews with the comparison group were to have been conducted during the month of June, 1977. However, because of the obstacles inherent in gaining access to a high school for research purposes and because of the fact that end-term exams and New York State Regents exams are both administered in June, the comparison sample was not selected and interviewed until October and November, 1977.

A screening procedure was established so that thirty comparison cases were selected and interviewed at Suburban High, a high school located on the north shore of Long Island. In order to have a simple random sample, the statistical independence of the adolescents in the comparison sample was required; the selection of each youth could not depend on the selection of any other youth. To insure statistical independence of selections, a table of random numbers was utilized. The names of forty-five adolescents were selected in equal numbers from the tenth, eleventh and twelfth grades. The first thirty teenagers who agreed to participate were interviewed. To find thirty participants, a total of forty-one youths was contacted. Of the eleven refusing to be interviewed, four were tenth graders, and three were twelfth graders. A sub-sample was interviewed to determine whether or not a congruence existed between the responses of the non-runaways and their parents.

OPERATIONAL DEFINITIONS

Two operational definitions have been delineated for this study: A runaway is a youth under eighteen years of age who leaves home without the consent of his/her parent(s) or guardian and is absent for at least twenty-four hours. Runaways include "throwaways," youths whose parents tell them to leave or physically eject them from the home. A crisis is primarily the encountering of one or more stressful events. The stressful event is perceived by the individual as leading to considerable upset and disruption, and the individual is unable to resolve the disruption by previously used coping mechanisms.

THE INFORMAL INTERVIEW

An informal approach for interviewing was used because it is generally accepted as best suited for researchers who are concerned with determining the respondents' views of situations, feelings and meanings (Nachmias and Nachmias, 1976: 101-102). An interview guide was selected (see Appendix I) rather than an interview schedule because of the flexibility of a guide. The interview guide enabled the researcher to explore various areas in depth with receptive respondents, while shortening interviews with a few respondents who seemed to be losing patience and interest and re-interviewing them at another time. On several occasions, the order of questions in the interview guide was altered to facilitate a thorough response from respondents.

A detailed interview guide was devised in order to gather data on the stressful experiences and background characteristics of the runaways. Background information, age, sex, race, family structure and the most frequent type of parental discipline were obtained. Respondents were asked about stress and coping, stressful life events occurring within the past four years, methods of coping with stress and crisis, the incident triggering a runaway act, and the typological categories of parent-youth conflict. Cognitive strengths and weaknesses may well compensate for or offset stressful events, and they were examined in terms of the youths' attitudes toward school, leisure-time activities, and anticipated life goals within the next five years. On the runaway episode itself, data were collected on a respondents' destination, problems encountered while on the run, and people who were considered either helpful or harmful to the runaways.

CHECKS AND CONTROL ON RETROSPECTIVE DATA

Many retrospective studies of adolescents, including adolescent runaways, have assumed that reports by the subjects under investigation combined with agency records yielded the best possible data. Rarely were systematic attempts made to assess or validate the information reported.

Because the runaway sample was asked to reconstruct the events, situations, and feelings which had often occurred several days, weeks, or even months prior to the interviews, it was important to assess the reliability of the runaways' perceptions with data from another source. Consequently, every effort was made to interview the parent(s) or guardian of the youths both in the runaway and comparison samples to determine the degree of agreement of parents' perceptions with the youths' perceptions.

Agency administrators are often resistant to allowing their clients' participation in research studies, because they fear that respondents' rights to privacy and confidentiality might be abused. They also may feel threatened by an "outside" researcher studying the workings of the agency and its clients. Such resistance was evident during this study.

LIMITATIONS OF THE STUDY

The generalizing of the findings in this study to other areas should be made cautiously. The study was based on a small sample of sixty youths — thirty runaways and thirty non-runaways. Because the runaway sample consisted of youths who had sought or were referred for professional counseling, they may not be representative of all runaway adolescents in crisis. The sample did not include adolescents who would not have accepted such treatment or who would have gone to a private therapist. The sample may also not be representative of all suburban youths because very few runaways chose New York City as their destination. Finally, it was not feasible to include those youths who fled from Long Island to out-of-state locations and did not return, because of the confidentiality of juvenile records, traveling expenses, and the prohibitive time required to find those youths.

IV. The Adolescents and The Perceptions of Discipline and Stress

AGE AND RACE

All of the subjects were white and from middle-class backgrounds. Social class is commonly measured in terms of occupation, education level attained, amount of income, and style of living. When viewed as a style of living, social class is defined by the goods and services a family consumes (Horton and Hunt, 1976:239). The sixty adolescents in this study were viewed as middle-class because all of the youths came from homogeneous neighborhoods on the North Shore of eastern Long Island, and all but four lived in affluent private homes. Therefore, social class was not considered to be a major variable, as it would have been, for example, in a study of the diverse populations of New York City or Queens County.

All but two of the runaways and two of the non-runaways lived in private homes rather than apartments.

The mean age for the thirty runaways was 15.76; the mean age for the thirty non-runaways was 16.03. In D'Angelo's (1974) Columbus, Ohio study, he reported a very similar mean age for runaways of 15.9 years. The youngest runaway interviewed was thirteen years old while two-thirds of the runaways sampled were sixteen or seventeen years old. In twelve cases, the runaways were sixteen years old, eight of the runaways were seventeen, six were fifteen and three were fourteen years of age.

Data describing runaway rates nationally indicate an increase in the number of young adolescent runaways in the thirteen to fourteen (Bayh, 1974:159) and twelve to sixteen (Raab, Oct. 30 and Nov. 2, 1977) age brackets. However, this data should be regarded cautiously because the data were based on police statistics. The parents of younger runaways may be more likely to report them as missing persons to the police, and the police, in turn, may be more likely to arrest younger children rather than the less visible sixteen and seventeen year olds who look like they may be eighteen years old.

SEX

The girls in the runaway sample seem to have left home or sought help more frequently than boys. The female-male ratio was 2.1 or twenty girls and ten boys. The finding concurs with earlier studies (Goldmeier and Dean, 1973; Foster, 1962; and Myers, 1977).

The comparison group's 2:1 ratio of twenty girls to ten boys occurred because eleven of the non-runaways, nine of whom were males, refused to be interviewed. Female non-runaway adolescents were more willing than boys to be interviewed. The boys' reluctance may have been caused by their feelings that participating in social work research was non-masculine or because they did not want to give of their time to a project that had no apparent meaning for them. Only three runaways refused to be interviewed — two were girls and one was a boy.

FAMILY STRUCTURE

The data were analyzed to compare runaways with non-runaways coming from both intact and non-intact homes. An intact family structurally consists of two natural parents at the time of the interview. In this study, almost half of the runaways came from "broken" or reconstituted homes, whereas only one in five of the non-runaways were from "broken" families. A broken home is defined as one in which there has been disruption due to death, divorce, separation or desertion or there is a single parent who has never married. A reconstituted family is defined as one in which the parent, who has custody of the minor, has remarried, resulting in a step-parent entering the home.

It was found that adolescents who came from broken or reconstituted homes were over-represented in the runaway group. Almost half or fourteen of the thirty runaways came from some form of broken (twelve) or reconstituted (four) home. Consequently, the likelihood of youths running away seems to increase when the natural family is not intact. This finding is in accord with Shellow, et.al.'s (1967) study in which forty-eight percent of the runaways came from non-intact homes, while only eighteen percent of the comparison sample came from a broken or reconstituted home.

PARENTAL DISCIPLINE

Data were collected on parents' disciplinary practices to obtain background information about the runaways' and non-runaways' family relationships. The quality of the parent-youth relationship is revealed to some extent by the youths' reporting of the type of parental discipline most frequently employed. Respondents were asked to cite the type of discipline most frequently administered by their parents or guardians. In the runaway group corporal punishment was used to a considerably greater extent than in the non-runaway group. One-half of the runaways reported that they had been hit, slapped, or beaten, as compared to only two of the thirty non-runaways. One possible explanation for this finding is that it may have been due to respondent biases. To illustrate, if a youth has not been labeled in a negative way, as a runaway often is, he or she may tend to give answers which show the family and self in a good light. Conversely, if a runaway already perceives himself or herself as "bad" or having family problems, then there may be a tendency to report and emphasize those aspects of their background which make their "bad" behavior understandable.

When asked whether their parents disciplined them, and if so to identify the type of discipline used most frequently, seventeen runaways indicated that their parents use yelling, fifteen indicated corporal punishment, seven indicated "grounding," four stated that their parents threatened to send them to the children's shelter. The non-runaways reported the following types of discipline: "talking things out" (fourteen respondents), yelling (thirteen), criticizing (seven), and corporal punishment (two).

Corporal punishment: The responses of the fifteen runaways and two non-runaways who received corporal punishment vary as much as their attitudes toward being hit. The runaways perceived their beatings as brutal, unfair, and undeserved. The abuse took place either in a one-parent family or in a family in which the non-abusing parent did not intervene or restrain the abusive parent in any way. In one instance both parents of the adolescent joined together in beating the youth.

In the runaway group, physical abuse by parents was evidenced by the following remarks:

I came home two hours late. He beat me with a two by four. I had all black marks.

— A fifteen-year-old girl.

All I remember is it was right before Christmas (seven months prior to the interview), and he was drunk and slapping me again and again.

— A sixteen-year-old girl.

When I was fifteen I only stole ten dollars out of her purse and she beat the piss out of me.

— A seventeen-year-old girl.

The adolescents in the runaway sample appeared reticent about reporting their parents' physically abusive behavior to the authorities for fear of reprisal. The experience of a fifteen-year-old girl vividly illustrates this fear:

> I was throwing up all day, and went to the school nurse. She told me I had a concussion. The nurse touched my nose and it hurt. She felt it and said it was cracked. She asked what happened. I told her I had a fight with some girl. She kept asking me questions and said for a very young girl she hit pretty hard. Finally I broke down and told her it was my father. She wanted to call the office or someone for child abuse. I wouldn't let her. My father would kill me if I reported him. I was dizzy and I couldn't see straight. I was off balance. She sent me home and called my father and told him to call the hospital.

The two non-runaways who reported that their parents used corporal punishment came from intact families in which one parent — the mother — was the youth's ally in trying to restrain the father's actions. Unlike the runaways, the non-runaways displayed an attitude of acceptance of the physical punishment as a response which they deserved because of some wrongdoing. These teenagers also expressed perceptions as to whether the parent really cared about their well-being and whether the corporal punishment resulted from that caring.

Paul, a non-runaway, accepted punishment from his father, even if it was sometimes corporal punishment:

> If I came home late by an hour, or I talked back to him because he was wrong, he started screaming and punching me. If I tried to hide behind a chair, it would be worse. He would get angrier and hit more in the stomach.

Paul believed that although his parents were strict, they cared about him. He said, "I know they care. My father thinks he's helping me." Paul's mother is also strict, but she sides with him when his father starts hitting Paul. One of the major arguments between Paul and his parents involved his participating in sports and acting in the school play. The parents were concerned that these activities would keep him from studying. Paul, having made a mutually acceptable arrangement with his mother said, "I sort of guaranteed that I will keep my grades up as long as I can get to rehearsals, choir practice two nights a week and play in intramurals."

Another non-runaway who reported occasional corporal punishment was Pat, age sixteen. She also seemed to accept her father's actions:

> Last year my mother was really upset because she thought I was acting like a bitch. She was crying and saying I had to change. My father got violent. He slapped me again and again.

On another occasion, Pat said,

> I got caught cutting a class and cheating on a test and that was pretty lousy. My mother tried to stop him from slapping me. I think I deserved it.

Grounding: Almost one-quarter or seven of the runaways reported that "grounding" was used as a means of discipline; only one non-runaway reported grounding as a discipline. Grounding is being confined to the house for a particular period of time, which in all but one case meant after school hours and on weekends. From the runaway group only one girl, who was grounded, was allowed visits by her friends. In all of the other cases, the teenagers were not permitted to have any friends visiting. Runaways reported considerable variation in the ways parents imposed grounding. Four youths said that they were grounded for a period of between several days and a week; one said that is was for three weeks; and two reported that grounding was imposed for an indefinite time period.

Five of the seven runaways said that they did not view grounding as an effective form of discipline because it was unfair since their friends did "worse" things and never were grounded, and because the punishment was ineffective parents were not consistent. The youths said grounding would last for a week or longer, but after a day or so the youths knew that the punishment would be forgotten. One sixteen year-old boy knew from experience that his parents did not follow-through on their threats:

> Mother tells me I'm grounded for three months and can't go out at all at night. Father tells me I stay out until 9:00 and grounding will be for two weeks. I stayed in for three days.

The father of one fifteen year-old girl kept her out of school so that he could supervise her activities the entire day:

> My father grounded me for three weeks — no phone calls, no music, no TV — for getting stoned. When he went to work I had to go to work with him. I was not allowed to eat with them [natural father and live-in girlfriend]. I had to eat in my room and then do the dishes. I had to go to work with him for five days and do secretarial work so he could watch me.

Talking, Explaining and/or Admonishing: Although talking about misbehavior is a form of discipline which was reported by fourteen of the non-runaways, it was not mentioned once by the runaways. The non-runaways reported that their parents often explained to them why they were upset, angry, or disappointed. In families in which one parent scolded or yelled, the other parent seemed to provide a calming influence and an ability to discuss his or her feelings about the youth's wrongdoing. A sixteen year-old girl said,

> They always talk to me about it. They try to understand why I behave in certain ways.

Carol, aged seventeen lived with her natural father and step-mother. She mentioned that talking things over is the only type of discipline used by her father.

> He trusts me. If I came in late, he might be mad and sometimes he might yell a little, but usually he understands and discusses things with me.

Freddy, aged fifteen, lived with his mother and his younger sister. Although his parents have been separated for more than a year, his father visits Freddy and the family an average of twice a week and seems to have a good relationship with his son. Freddy described his father's approach to a problem:

> He would talk to me and make the point and ya know, he would give an example. He's logical when he tells me something.

Freddy wants to do well in school so that he can get into a good college and become an accountant. He feels that his father understands him, and he understands that his father would like him to do well in school. Freddy said:

> He is like me. He didn't do that well in school. He would goof off in his room when he was supposed to be studying. He would like me to do well.

Withholding Privileges: A parent's withholding or threatening to withhold privileges was reported by seven of the non-runaways, compared to nine of the runaways. Removal of privileges usually meant limiting the youths' television viewing time on week nights, the mother's refusing to drive the youngster to a sports event or friend's house, or withholding allowance for one to two weeks. A parent's refusal to drive their son or daughter to a destination of importance would seem to be an especially effective punishment in a suburban area because the public transportation system in that area was limited at best.

Criticizing: Parental criticism was reported by seven of the non-runaways and by only one of the runaways. Criticizing ranged from name-calling and beating to actual concern about the youth's future well-being. The following two examples illustrate parental criticism:

> If you don't do your homework you will never amount to anything. It's getting harder and harder to get into college.

And:

> Whenever they don't understand me or I swear, they tell

me I am rotten and no good.

Evelyn, at sixteen years of age, does well academically with a ninety-two average. Although she often reads, plays the piano, and paints in her leisure time, she described her father as being petty and faultfinding in his reproaches of her:

> My father never reveals his true feelings towards anyone or about anything. He may pick on stupid trivial things or criticize me in some way just as an outlet.

Evelyn reported having a good relationship with her mother and it seems that their bond serves to counteract her father's negativism.

Silent Treatment: Three runaways and one non-runaway indicated that their parents were advocates of the "silent treatment" as a form of discipline. Lauri, the one non-runaway whose parents use silence as discipline, felt that her parents were usually lenient with her. When they do discipline her, they impose silence and withhold her allowance. According to Lauri, her mother would explain the purpose of the punishment:

> I didn't like what you did, so I won't talk to you. When you show us that you can be responsible and come home on time or call to explain the delay, we will talk and give you your weekly allowance.

Lauri indicated that as a result of the discipline she felt guilty for having disobeyed her parents.

The runaways' parents who used silent treatment did not explain the purpose and duration of the punishment; instead they made derogatory statements like, "You worthless bitch, I'm sick of talking to you."

V. Adolescents in Stress and Coping with Crisis

To date, no researcher has assessed the stressful precipitating events that contribute to an unsteady state of crisis among adolescent runaways. This vulnerable and hazardous state of crisis can be characterized by anxiety, confusion, disorientation, fear, and depression which may lead to avoidance activities like frequent crying and sleeping, as well as escapist behavior like drug use, drinking and running away.

Comparative analysis of the type and number of stressful events in the lives of runaways and non-runaways: An important question arises as to whether or not runaways experienced more stressful events or more disintegrative events than did the non-runaways. Data were analyzed for the last four years for eighteen categories of personal and family stress. Analysis revealed that it was usually not a particular stressful event in an adolescent's life that led him or her to run away; it was the type and number of events that were the important factors.

Although assessment of stressful events were confined to the relatively recent past, many of the youths seemed unable to verbalize the meaning each event had had for them. This finding concurs with Hansell's (1976: 25-26) documentation that a common pattern among his clients in crisis was that they had filtered "random memory recall." Aguilera and Messick (1974:67) have also stated that individuals in crisis may not have a conscious awareness of the stressful events which led to their crisis. To help determine whether or not the perceptions of the runaways and non-runaways were selective, reliability of perceptions was validated in interviews with parents (see Chapter VI).

Findings indicate that instead of one isolated event precipitating a runaway act, several stressful events cumulatively seemed to result in an adolescent's running away. Specifically, a total of 130 or an average of 4.33 stressful events were experienced by each of the thirty runaways during the four years preceeding the interviews. However, the thirty non-runaways experienced a total of only seventy-six or an average of 2.53 stressful events during the same period. Although twenty-one of the runaways had encountered three or more stressful events during the years 1973 to 1977, thirteen of the thirty non-runaways each had experienced three or more stressful events, yet they did not run away from home.

Crisis theorists have viewed "crises" as transitional periods which either provide the individual with an opportunity for personal growth or result in emotional deterioration (Caplan, 1964; and Parad and Caplan, 1960). An individual in crisis reaches a "peak or sudden turning point" (Parad and Caplan, 1960) when tension increases to stimulate the mobilization of previously hidden strengths and capacities. Of eighteen kinds of stressful events, six kinds of stress were determined for which the number of non-runaways reporting was equal to or greater than the number of runaways. However, the non-runaways did not exhibit disintegrative behavior; they did not frequently use hallucinogens or alcohol or run away from home. Consequently, rather than crisis events routinely having a disintegrative effect, they may prove to be growth enhancing and integrative instead.

Generally the stress-producing events experienced by the non-runaways did not have a disintegrative effect, while the

cumulative effect of stressful events experienced by the
runaways did have a disintegrative effect.

An analysis of the ratio of stress-producing events reported
by the runaways indicates that the following six stresses were
encountered only by the runaways:

1. beaten by parent;
2. parent's lover moves into house;
3. thrown out of the home;
4. death of a parent;
5. youth was caught dealing in drugs; and
6. youth placed in children's shelter.

These stresses contributed to strained family relations and
maladaptive behavior on the part of the runaways. In contrast,
the following six stresses did not have maladaptive consequences for the non-runaways experiencing them:

1. serious illness or hospitalization of youth;
2. serious illness or hospitalization of parent;
3. parent's remarriage;
4. youth's broken romance;
5. death of a grandparent;
6. miscellaneous stresses.

Although these stresses did not have a disintegration effect
upon non-runaways, these stresses were reported in either equal
numbers by the two groups, or more frequently by the non-
runaways.

*Stress and crisis in non-intact homes: Selected runaway il-
lustrations:* There are often two aspects to the stress resulting
from the loss of a parent, there is the loss itself, through death,
divorce or separation and there is the way the rest of the family
copes with that loss. Stressful situations which arise *after* a
death or divorce can be as traumatic, if not more so, to an adolescent than the actual death or separation. During several interviews with runaway youths who had lost a parent through
death, it became apparent that the remaining parent was blaming the child for the death. The removal of a member of a social

system like a family had apparently changed the smoothness
with which the family functioned and the power relationships
among its members.

Frankie and Mike said they had had a close relationship with
their fathers, but the grief over their fathers' deaths was being
exacerbated by their respective mothers' verbal harrassment.
Frankie reported that he was shocked by his father's sudden
heart attack and death, adding that his mother not only did
nothing to help him with his grief but rather blamed him for the
death:

> My mother always tells me the I [slight pause] killed my
> father. That it's all my fault. And then she gives me the shit
> that. . .she'd rather me dead instead of my father. And they
> [the Department of Social Services] want to send me back
> there. They think that's a cool place for me to stay. Really,
> I'd rather be dead than have to go back to that place, back to
> my house, ya know. It's like so fucked up. I'd love to be sent
> to a foster home. My mother won't let me go. I'd rather go to
> jail or kill myself. . . . It's like being dead living at my house
> anyway. She treats me like she loves me when people are
> around, but really she's just out to fuck me up.

Mike had a history of being abused; he was physically abused
by his natural parents during the first three years of his life.
Before the age of eight, he had lived in three different foster
homes where he was also physically abused and neglected. His
medical history includes a spleenectomy, the suspected cause of
which was severe beatings during his childhood. Mike was
adopted at the age of eight-and-a-half. He said that he developed
a good relationship with his adoptive father, who died of cirrhosis of the liver four years ago. According to Mike, his adoptive mother became depressed, morbid, and constantly
attacked Mike in emotionally and physically violent ways,
blaming him for the step-father's death. Mike became an
alcoholic, and at the age of fourteen, he spent ten months confined to the adolescent unit of a psychiatric hospital for his
alcoholism and emotional problems. Upon release, he did not
want to return home, and his psychiatrist recommended that an

alternative living arrangement be sought. When the case was referred to the Department of Social Services and a caseworker met with Mike's mother, the mother refused to sign the permission release which would have allowed him to be removed from the home.

During the past seventeen months, Mike had runaway five times. He talked about his most recent experience:

> She told me to get out. Yelling and throwing things at me. She kept saying "You killed your father." I ran to my friend. They let me stay. I hid in the basement.

Mike said that he had stayed with his friend for five months. He got along well with his friend's father and helped them around the house.

Stressful situations can persist after a divorce, especially when both parents remain embittered and hostile toward each other. Lisa's parents were divorced. Lisa, a fifteen-year-old, had been living with her father, her two brothers aged twelve and nineteen, and her father's girlfriend. Lisa also had a twenty-one-year-old sister living on her own with a girlfriend. One night, Lisa's alcoholic mother came to visit. She had been drinking, and during an ensuing argument, the mother picked up a long kitchen knife and went after the father. Lisa left the house and went to stay with her sister. Lisa's departure was her first runaway act. Lisa indicated that she ran away the second time because her father was continually yelling at her and giving orders. She said, "He wants me to clean up after him, to cook and clean everyday." Two interviews were held with Lisa's father. He appeared to have been drinking heavily before the second interview, which was especially informative because it became apparent that the man was projecting onto his children the anger he had had towards his girlfriend who had left him after an eighteen-month liaison. He said,

> Oh, I understand them [his children]. I think they don't understand me. So there. We're even. That's where the communication comes in. We don't understand each other. I

don't understand their, uh, attitude towards parents or other people, ya know, like when we were children.

He was asked, "How do you feel about the attitude of many kids today that they want to do their own thing?" He replied:

We did our own thing too when we were young but in a different way. We still had respect for our parents, ya know. But today, that's why I holler because I'm getting nowheres at times, ya know. I don't get respect. If I say something, I want it this way, I want it that way which I think I have a right, it most of the time don't happen the way I want it, and this is why I get bitter at em. I guess maybe sometimes it might be a childish thing of mine, although I can't have my way, ya know, but it isn't all that. When my girlfriend left I started picking on the kids more. I took it out on the kids. I practically said it was their fault. This is why I picked on the kids. I blamed the kids.

Stress in non-intact homes: Non-runaway illustrations: Carol, Freddy, and Janis each experienced the stress of their parent's separation and divorce, compounded by additional stresses like an alcoholic parent, a move from a familiar neighborhood, and frequent arguments with the remaining parent or sibling. However, these youths did *not* run away from home.

Carol's mother had been an alcoholic. Her parents divorced nine years ago when Carol was eight. Carol and her older sister have lived with the father, with whom Carol has developed a close relationship. During the past two years, Carol has had to deal with her newly married sister and brother-in-law living in her home. She found the situation particularly stressful:

My father was never home and with his girlfriend. I was jealous. I had a lot of stress because of my brother-in-law. His sense of everything is different from us. He is from Italy. I felt very uncomfortable. I also had a lot of stress from my sister. She would always put me down in front of him [the brother-in-law].

With her father's permission, Carol left an unbearable situation to live with an aunt for a year. Then she stayed with her
mother, who stopped drinking, and step-father for five months.
Carol then returned to live with her father. Carol did not live at
her father's home for almost a year-and-a-half, but she would
not be considered a runaway because she left home with her
father's permission. The transition from one home to another
was planned ahead of time; all parties involved agreed to the
move which was accomplished without Carol's acting and feeling like a fugitive.

The parents of Freddy, aged fifteen, were divorced a few
months ago. During the past four years, the family had moved
three times. The final move, occurring when his parents
separated, upset Freddy because it separated him from some
close friends. However, he continued to frequently telephone his
friends from his former neighborhood which was approximately
twenty-five miles away. Before the divorce, Freddy and his
father had been especially close, and their relationship was
maintained after the separation through telephone calls and his
father's visits approximately twice a week. Freddy reported
that when his parents separated he was quite upset and his
grade average dropped from a ninety to an eighty-two. He said,
"It was a bad scene. I couldn't work. I goofed off." With his
father gone, he also found it difficult getting along with his
mother:

> When my father left, she [mother] would cry and cry and
> would pick on me. Then I would retaliate and there was a
> whole scene. There were times when she would say, "Go live
> with your father."

Freddy felt that as a result of the divorce he has become a
more responsible person. He was asked, "Have you ever
thought about running away from home?" He replied, "No.
Why would you want to leave your security [where] you have
food and music and everything."

When her parents separated, Janis and her younger brother

stayed with their mother. Her father had been an alcoholic, and a few weeks before her parents separated, the father's hair styling business went bankrupt. Before the separation, the family lived in a large single family home in a fashionable neighborhood and were well-off financially. Failing to have realized that the father's bankruptcy, even if the family had stayed together, would have meant a change in their life style, Janis resented the loss of the house, the end of their former standard of living, and the fact that her mother had to go to work. Because of impending financial difficulties, Janis' mother began working full-time a year before the father's business loss. To Janis, her father was the guilty party:

> I've resented my father. Then I feel guilty cause you shouldn't. But we used to have a lot of money, now we don't so I resent it. And I see my mother working and we're living in a garden apartment.

Janis has a vague recollection of her father's alcoholism. When the father was drunk, his wrath was apparently directed more at his wife than at his children because Janis said she did not remember the father's having been bad to her. However, she does recall his having a "foul mouth" with her mother. About a year ago, Janis came home drunk and her mother was furious. She said her mother "had a fit. She hit me and I went to bed." However, Janis does not bear her mother any ill will for hitting her:

> She hit me in anger. My father used to drink so I can see why she was upset when I was drinking.

Janis said that she has never considered running away from home. Her mother's difficult financial circumstances following the separation seem to have served to heighten the girl's awareness of the importance of budgeting and money management. Janis' ability to cope with the divorce seems to be sustained by her close relationship with her mother, which has grown stronger since the divorce. Janis feels good that she and her mother can confide in each other.

Crisis in intact homes: Runaway illustrations: Crisis in the lives of adolescents is not confined to situations arising from broken homes. Lynn, Peter, and Kathy were three runaway youths who were growing up in homes where their parents' marriages were legally intact but where the families were experiencing major stresses.

Lynn, aged seventeen, had three runaway episodes. Lynn mentioned that her father had been unemployed for five months. She said the first runaway experience occurred because her parents grounded her for one week because of her relationship with her boyfriend:

> My parents made me break-up with my boyfriend who I was going with for four months. I told them I did but I really didn't. It's on my mind constantly. I despise my parents for it and will always hold it against them.

Lynn had been grounded again for coming home two hours past her curfew. When her parents imposed what she considered to be an unfair punishment, Lynn ran away. Lynn reported that her father's slapping her for failing two subjects in school led to her "splitting" again six weeks later. According to Lynn:

> My father's always on my back for bad language and yelling at them [her parents]. I always get punished or smacked in the face.

Peter described the ambience in his home — his father's illness and subsequent conversion to strong religious beliefs — which led to his leaving:

> Last year, my father had an operation on his spine for a pinched nerve or something. Now he has fifty percent use of his right arm, a slipped disc and he is two inches shorter. Now they changed to Jesus this and Jesus that. They go to prayer meetings all the time. When I had a disagreement with my father he tried to turn me into a Jesus freak. He is always searching my room for pot, and grounding me. My

mother tells me to search my heart — "You're a sinner and must be punished."

Arguments over religious beliefs entered into the stresses with which two runaways had to deal; however, for Peter, it was his parents who became fervent believers while he remained a skeptic.

For Kathy, she demonstrated a keen interest in religion while her parents doubted her sincerity. Kathy was one of the runaways who revealed that they were in a perpetual state of crisis, characterized by continual, destructive family conflict and tension. Kathy's father had been awarded many medals for his work as a New York City policeman. Unfortunately, according to Kathy, he was an alcoholic and when he was at home he was constantly criticizing and harrassing her. Although Kathy received above average grades in school, she felt as though she was being "brainwashed" because her parents had repeatedly told her she was lazy. When the family visited relatives, Kathy overheard her parents telling them that she was lazy and "throws temper tantrums." Kathy, the eldest of six children, perceptively summarized what she felt was the underlying source of conflict between her and her parents:

He [father] would make fun of me for reading books. He dropped out of high school. I am scholastically good. . .He's mean to me because I didn't grow parallel to him. All the kids are signed up for Little League. I never signed up. They all go for karate lessons with my father. They will do anything daddy will do. I don't like that stuff. . .They [her parents] don't believe in what I am. I was taking religion classes. They thought I did it to impress neighbors. They don't believe in church. They would do it only for their neighbors.

Kathy experienced further stress because her mother seems to be displacing onto her daughter the pent-up anger the mother feels toward her husband. In Kathy's words:

He calls my mother an ugly old hag and says he wants to

leave her. He has a girlfriend from time to time. A few years ago, he introduced me to his girlfriend that works at Macy's. She [her mother] would slap me and hit me. The last time she hit me over the head with her shoe. When I got up from the floor, I kicked her, hit her and ran out.

During the first runaway episode, Kathy slept at her girlfriend's house for one night. About two months later Kathy ran away again to another friend's house but came home by herself the next day. The arguments between her and her parents persisted. Finally, Kathy went to her school guidance counselor who referred her to the local youth counseling center. The center placed her in a temporary foster home for two days and encouraged her and her parents to try to live together again. Within a week, Kathy's parents sent her to New Jersey to live with her grandparents; she stayed there for sixteen months. At the time of the interview Kathy had been living at her girlfriend's house for the past eight months with her parents' permission. Both she and her mother were participating in psychotherapy at the same clinic. Her father had refused to participate in therapy. Kathy described how she was trying to cope with the multiple stresses in her life:

I wouldn't hear them. I would turn off. I would think of good days that made me happy — if I made a new friend, if I went out with someone to a movie and had a really good time. If I know they are going to fight with me, I would avoid it and go talk to a friend about it. Sometimes I would fight back or try to talk it out. If my mother started screaming and hitting, I would try and get out and go to a girlfriend's.

Kathy's family conflicts seem to be of a higher intensity than those of most non-runaways; however, her coping mechanisms do not appear to be too dissimilar from those of some of the non-runaways in stress. Kathy had temporarily alleviated the family conflict and stress by staying with a friend when one or both parents became violent toward her. The main difference between Kathy and some of the non-runaways is that initially she did not have parental permission when she was gone overnight. Ultimately, she did receive parental permission for lengthy stays at her grandparents' house and at a friend's house.

Two illustrations of non-runaways from intact homes under heavy stresses: JoAnn and Sheila, who were both very talkative girls provided detailed information on two youths from intact homes who have experienced much stress yet did not run away and seemed to have adapted to their respective circumstances.

JoAnn, age sixteen, has had to cope with a number of stresses. She is the youngest of three children, all of whom live at home. She has a sister, aged twenty-one, who is a senior at a nearby college and with whom she has a very close relationship. Her brother, aged thirty, is mentally retarded and works as a custodian. JoAnn's mother has had four major heart attacks; the first attack occurred when JoAnn was ten years old, necessitating the girl's living with an aunt for two months. The mother's most recent heart attack occurred during the summer of 1976. Approximately three-and-a-half years ago the mother was rushed to the hospital because of a "lump" in her head which was later diagnosed as a blood clot.

JoAnn felt that her mother is nervous and nags at her constantly, saying, "Don't go outside without a coat. Get you coat. Don't forget ya key. You sure you have your key?"

JoAnn has had a history of severe migraines, and two years ago was hospitalized for two weeks for a series of grueling diagnostic tests (e.g. EEG, X-Rays, spinal tap) could be performed. She recalls that one test was particularly difficult to bear:

[I] couldn't tolerate the dye. They gave me a red dye to take. I would get dizzy and nauseous. They would bring me back to bed and make me try again the next day.

The tests proved negative. She still suffers from the migraines.

JoAnn's closs relationship with her older sister was reinforced when JoAnn had missed many classes because of mononucleosis. JoAnn's history teacher had said that she was going to fail the history course because of poor grades and too many absences. At the time, JoAnn's mother was in the hospital and JoAnn's sister served as her advocate by going to school to speak to the history teacher and the principal. As a result, JoAnn received a passing grade.

According to JoAnn, whenever she has a problem, she talks with her sister and "analyzes it" on her own. She said she has never considered running away. Her reaction to stress may be to internalize it thereby developing migraine headaches; other youths externalize stress by running away from their problems. Several experts in the field have viewed migraines as a psychosomatic condition resulting from negative emotion and stress (Lachman, 1972: 85; and McQuade and Aikman, 1974: 39-40).

Sheila, aged seventeen has a mother who has had part of her stomach and spleen removed due to an ulcer; she had been hospitalized for five weeks. Her father's business went bankrupt approximately three years ago, and he was unemployed for approximately seven months. A year ago, a friend of Sheila was killed in a motorcycle accident. The whole family was subjected to stress when Sheila's grandmother moved into their home because she was ill with cancer. The family witnessed her steadily weakening condition and her death two years later.

Sheila said that she and her mother had frequent arguments, mainly about her boyfriend. She felt that her mother was "always blaming Steve [the boyfriend] for what I do." The mother is also upset by the sexual relationship between Sheila and Steve, having said on more than one occasion to her daughter, "Why don't you just go and live with him!" Her parents want her to spend more time with the family, away from her boyfriend. When she and her parents engage in one of their arguments, Sheila says of her parents' response:

> They think they brought me up wrong. Whenever they don't understand, they just say that I'm rotten.

Sheila said that she had thought about running away from

home because of her mother's "picking on" her. However, she "reasons" to herself that runing away "won't solve my problem. It will always be there when I get back." To deal with frustration and stress, she said she tries to:

> reason with myself; try and break down the problem. Tell myself that I'm going to be what I want to be.

She also confides in her boyfriend and tries to be away from the conflict as much as possible during the day by being very active in school activities. She also worked several days a week as a cashier in a local supermarket.

COPING SKILLS

An individual is normally able to maintain a balance between inner tensions and outer stresses through the use of familiar behavioral patterns. Everyone encounters stresses in everyday living, but in most cases these stresses are resolved by various previously learned methods of problem-solving and coping. When an individual is involved in an intolerable situation which cannot be resolved by previously learned methods of coping, that individual may rapidly proceed to a state of crisis.

Coping can be regarded as a process of adaptive behavior calling for the mastery of new situations involving potential threat, challenge, or gratification (Coelho, et. al., Lazarus, Murphy, and White). Coping is defined as the "problem solving efforts made by an individual" when that individual encounters a situation which is potentially threatening and considerably taxing to his or her resources (Lazarus, et. al., 1974: 250-251).

An examination was made of the ways by which both runaway and non-runaway adolescents coped with stressful or threatening situations. It became apparent that an overwhelming majority of the non-runaways used coping mechanisms to maintain a steady or balanced state. These non-runaways successfully used problem-solving methods to cope with stress. They maintained an interpersonal closeness with a significant other individual like a close relative, an older sibling, or a professional counselor. Finally, they did not use drugs like cocaine,

PCP, and LSD.

The thirty runaways were asked: "When you experience a stressful situation or heavy problem, is there any way that you can help yourself?" All of the runaways answered affirmatively "yes." When asked: "In what ways can you help yourself?" — the overwhelming majority (25) reported that they help themselves by taking drugs or alcohol (9 runaways), leaving the house temporarily (4), crying (4), attempting suicide (2), going to sleep (2), trying to forget it (2), and running away (2). Only five runaways seemed to try to cope with threatening situations by talking with another individual about their problems.

Runaways described their negative escapist behavior:

> I've taken a bottle of aspirins and got sick, go out partying and slit my wrists when no one was home.
>
> — a fifteen-year-old girl.

> I go out of the house and I get very drunk.
>
> — a sixteen-year-old boy.

> I just try to mellow myself out. It's cool for the moment.
>
> — a fifteen-year-old boy.

The boy also indicated that he "turns on" with acid and has taken over 150 "trips." He said he smokes pot several times a week, and once in a while he snorted cocaine and takes "downs" with Darvon. He explained that he opens the Darvon capsules and empties three or four of them into his alcoholic drink.

In the runaway sample, eighty-three percent of the adolescents reported the use of maladaptive means for dealing with stress, but in the non-runaway group, the figure was reversed, and eighty percent or twenty-four non-runaways reported coping with stress by means of problem-solving processes. The non-runaways "think it through" (8 non-runaways); think about it and then talk to somebody about it (4); talk to a friend (6); talk to mother and also to friends (1); talk to mother (1); talk to older brother about the problem and do transcendental meditation (1); and write about it (3).

The non-runaways described the positive and adaptive problem-solving processes used in stressful situations:

> I think about it, and try to work it out on my own by getting things clear in me and talking to other people about it. Hear what they have to say.

> I write everything down in my diary. It helps whenever unhappy or sad emotions have to come out.

> Depending on the problem it sometimes helps to simply be alone and think and sometimes write. But at other times, when it's a big problem, I need to talk to someone else to help straighten out my real feelings about the situation, or simply for comfort and security.

A sixteen-year-old runaway girl felt it useful to talk to her mother or a friend when she had a problem:

> Even if they just listen, talking about it and thinking the problem out helps.

To determine whether running away is an adaptive or maladaptive method of coping, the following questions need to be asked: Did the runaways flee impulsively, before having tried some less drastic method of coping with their problems? Had they first attempted to resolve a problem by using previously learned methods of coping, and had they been unsuccessful?

The findings contrast the coping mechanisms runaways reported using prior to running with the adaptive methods successfully used by non-runaways. The majority — seventeen of the runaway youths — tried temporary avoidance by withdrawing, rebelling or leaving home temporarily, or positive problem-solving like thinking through the problem or talking to a friend. Eleven of the runaways used maladaptive escapist forms of behavior before running away. Of the eleven, two reported frequent pill-popping or heavy drinking and suicide attempts by wrist-slashing. The other nine frequently used drugs and excessive drinking. Two of the runaways reported using running away exclusively as their only method of coping.

Unlike the runaways, none of the non-runaways reported suicide attempts or running away as a form of coping. Only one reported drinking beer and other liquor and taking stimulants and LSD as a means of coping. This finding is important because it points out that generally both runaway and non-runaway adolescents seem reluctant to resort initially or exclusively to the most drastic forms of coping; they tended to first try previously learned coping mechanisms.

TRIGGERING INCIDENTS

All thirty of the runaways perceived that stress with one or both parents contributed to their running away. In addition to reporting precipitating stresses, the runaways provided information on the "last straw" which they felt had triggered their leaving home. Triggering incidents included being treated unfairly by a parent, beaten, yelled at, insulted, and thrown out of the house.

Ten of the thirty runaways indicated that they were being treated unfairly by their parent(s). Twelve runaway episodes were triggered by recurring arguments and conflict with parents. Parents usually yelled at their children but they also threw the youth's clothes on the floor, ripped the youth's posters off the wall, and destroyed personally valued records and tapes; in one case a mother was accused of "slamming doors" in her daughter's face. In six cases, the "last straw" was the pain of physical abuse, and in two cases it was the fear of another beating that triggered the runaway episode.

PHYSICAL ABUSE

Although half of the runaways indicated that their parents frequently disciplined them by hitting, slapping, or beating, only six youths said that recurring beatings by a parent had triggered their running away. A history of physical abuse may have led all of these runaways from their homes but most of them were not consciously aware of their resentment or did not verbalize it. Some youths may have exaggerated the frequency and magnitude of the physical discipline which their parents used, and they may have had a greater tolerance for physical rather then emotional pain and suffering.

Catherine, aged fourteen, related that having run away, she was living in a foster home. She spoke of how her father had repeatedly abused her:

> He started sexually abusing me. . . It's been happening since I was eleven years old, I guess because of my mother's high blood pressure. My brother Joey [younger brother] used to try and help me by crying. . . He [father] started me taking uppers, downers, acid. My mother never knew it. She was out. My father taught me if I told he would kill me. When I did bad in school he would keep me in at night and beat me. He kept hitting me in the stomach.

When Catherine ran away from home she stayed at a friend's house. For Catherine, running away seems to have been an adaptive way to survive.

Johnny, aged fifteen, had been living with his father for two years. His parents were divorced and his father who is an alcoholic, had thrown him to the ground and stomped on him until he was unconscious. To escape from the physical batterings which his drunken father would give him, Johnny ran away. During the day he roamed the streets and at night he slept wherever he found temporary shelter — in laundry rooms, bicycle rooms, and empty cars. When the father, suffering from liver damage, went to the hospital, Johnny's mother agreed to let the boy live with her.

Allison, aged fifteen, indicated that grounding for an indefinite period combined with the fear of further physical abuse triggered her running away. Allison's parents had been divorced for eight years. Before the divorce, her father had been arrested for beating his wife. Allison is the oldest of four children. Her three siblings are living with their natural mother who has remarried. However, for some unapparent reason, Allison was not wanted in her mother and step-father's home. Allison indicated that she ran the first and second times because her father did not want her to date boys until she was eighteen years old. When she had a boy friend, he refused to allow her to see him. Allison revealed that for the first two runaway acts she had gone to friends' houses and each time her father had found her within two to three days. Each time when he brought her home, he disciplined her with beatings and grounding her to her room.

Her third runaway episode was triggered when two students at school reported to the assistant principal that Allison was selling marijuana. The assistant principal brought Allison to his office, searched her purse, and found marijuana. He then called her home, and her father's girlfriend who was living at Allison's house took her home. When her father came home from work, he beat Allison as he had done on many previous occasions; he also imposed grounding for an indefinite period. She ran away at 2:30 that night. It seems that her third and final runaway act was triggered by her fear of further beatings and continued confinement to the house. She was living in a group home.

Unfair treatment: Runaways often described their parent's "unfair treatment." Melissa felt pressure to follow in her older sister's footsteps:

> Connie [her 18-year-old sister] and my mother get along so well. She's the super jock — basketball, field hockey, shot-put, track team. She wins trophies. She has my mother drive her all over. Straight A student. My mother and father don't like my attitude. My mother is my father's guide. He agrees to everything she wants. She tries to get me to go out for sports. I like being myself, I hate my mother. She told me she didn't love me anymore and threatened to send me to the children's shelter. She told me I made everyone uncomfortable. Super jock sister would agree.

Melissa perceived that her parents had been insensitive to the rivalry between her and her sister and had neglected Melissa's need for acceptance and the recognition of being loved for herself. Melissa's first runaway episode occurred when her parents had left for a weekend. Melissa told them she would be going to Wildwood, New Jersey on a class trip. Instead, she left home taking the train to New York City where she reported having overdosed on "downers." She was found by the police and taken to a hospital where she stayed for about a week. Upon her return home, conflict between her and her mother intensified. Melissa said her mother told her that she did not love Melissa anymore and threatend to call the police and charge her daughter with drug possession. The threats led to Melissa's second running away to a nearby friend's house. The friend's mother contacted Melissa's mother to tell her of the girl's whereabouts. Melissa was subsequently placed in a short-term group home for counseling because of her runaway behavior and her drug problem.

Donna reports that her parents severely restrict her freedom by refusing to allow her to spend time with her friends. Donna's father is an ex-alcoholic who spends his spare time at Alcoholics Anonymous meetings or with friends every night. Donna reports that when her overweight mother is not at her half-time job, she is involved with Overeaters Anonymous. Donna, at fifteen years of age, is required to babysit with her younger sister and two younger brothers almost every night, including weekends. Her mother will not let Donna invite friends to the house when she is babysitting. Donna said:

> My parents haven't been getting along and they have been taking it out on me. They were keeping me in a cage, and I couldn't get off the block and it all got to me and I took off.

Arguments: The arguments adolescents may have with their parents can vary greatly from one family to the next. Depending on the temperament and the nature and number of previous arguments, each new conflict may be intensified. Differing values and a lengthy period of a parent's being unemployed intensified arguments in two cases.

According to Tom, the arguments in his family concerned his relationship with his girlfriend:

> I started going out with Rochelle who is Jewish. They [his parents] would curse out all Jewish people. . . My father wouldn't let me out of the house. He was drinking and started punching away at me. I tried to push him away. He told the police he wants to press charges against me for harrassment. The police said he could press charges. I said I would press charges on him for child abuse. They said we should go to Family Court if we want. My parents wouldn't go. I was up all night fighting with my father.

The following day, Saturday, at 8:30 A.M., Tom left home.

In Rita's house her father has been unemployed for almost two years, and the teenager had witnessed her mother's anger and disparaging attitude toward her father. Rita said:

> My mother was screaming at me to put on a dress because people were coming to look at our house and no one is going to buy our house if I was dressed like a pauper. She came from a rich family and was used to luxury. My mother and father were fighting a lot. She would tell him, "How could you do this to me? A real man would be able to support his family." There was so much tension in the house because of financial difficulties. . . We started fighting and my mother said, "If you don't like living here, leave." I went to my cousin's house in the city [New York City] for two weeks. . . After the first week when my uncle came to see my cousin he found out I was there and told them [my parents] where I was. My mother called and apologized and said she wanted me to come home. I went home three days later.

PARENT-YOUTH CONFLICT CONTINUUM

In this study, the thirty runaways had three experiences in common; they had family-related problems; they experienced school failure, evidenced by failing courses, a history of missing classes, truancy, and being suspended; they frequently got "wasted" with drugs or drunk on alcohol. The extent of the runaways' problems in their families, in school, and with drugs is plotted on a continuum of parent-youth conflict among the thirty cases.

Figure I describes an emotional conflict continuum for runaways based on a five-point scale; the definition of each point is selective and limited to the data obtained from this suburban sample of clinic runaways.

FIGURE I
FORMULATION OF THE DEGREE OF
PARENT-YOUTH CONFLICT CONTINUUM

0	1+	2+	3+	4+
Non-Runaways	Runaway Explorers & Runaway Social Pleasure Seekers	Runaway Manipula-tors	Runaway Retreatists	Endangered Runaways

Zero to One Level — The non-runaways experience minimal conflict between parent and adolescent, and whatever conflict does occur is tolerated and resolved without the youth's becoming a runaway. Some youths may want to travel on their own or with a friend to assert their independence, but should a non-runaway be determined to travel, the parents would arrange a compromise and the youth's leaving home completely on his or her own would be averted. The type of compromise which is arranged depends to a great extent on the age of the teenager and the parents' perception of the capability and maturity of the youth. A compromise which may be acceptable to the parents of a seventeen-year-old may not be acceptable to the parents of a thirteen-year-old.

In this study, fourteen of the non-runaways indicated that they had been involved with their parents in compromise and mutual goal setting concerning a trip. Usually the parents insist that the youth get a part-time job to earn some or all of the money necessary to finance a trip; the parent might agree to match whatever the youth earns.

The parents may also suggest that the youth investigate supervised group travel which enables the youth to feel independence while still being chaperoned. Parents may encourage their youngsters to take "Teen Tours" or trips sponsored by schools, youth centers, church or synagogue youth groups. Youngsters may plan a trip with one or more close friends and receive parental permission for the journey.

Sometimes the parents may arrange for the youth to visit an out-of-town relative on his or her own or the whole family might take a trip together with the understanding that part of the time the youth will be free to explore an area on his or her own, returning to join the family for dinner or meeting back at the hotel in the evening.

Level 1+ — Runaway Explorers and Runaway Social Pleasure Seekers: The characteristics of Explorers were determined from interviews with two runaways who reported unfair treatment by their parents as the incident triggering their runaway episode. Additional information was obtained from the boyfriend of one girl in the study sample. He was an Explorer who had successfully left home for Florida, but he was not included in this study because he was not a client of Runaway Retreat. Explorers have a desire to travel alone or sometimes with a friend for adventure and to assert their independence. Usually the youth informs parents of the intention to travel, but the parents refuse to give permission because they feel the youth is too young for such an undertaking. The youth then leaves home without permission. Explorers generally leave their parents a note telling them that they have left, or they telephone their parents within twenty-four to forty-eight hours of departure to allay the parents' fears about their absence. The police are always looking for hitchiking teenagers who may be runaways. If not found by the police and returned promptly to their parents, Explorers generally contact their parents on their own and ask to return home whenever they have seen and done what they set out to do.

Social Pleasure Seekers: The characteristics of Social Pleasure Seekers emerged from interviews with four runaways in this study. Social Pleasure Seekers are usually girls who have had a conflict with their parents over what the girls think is an important issue like a restriction on dating a certain boy, an early Saturday night curfew, or a grounding which prevents them from going to a particular social event. Prior to the conflict, the girls often had a relatively good relationship with their parents, but on this one issue the girls are determined to have their own way. Social Pleasure Seekers generally sneak out of the house or leave under the pretext of visiting a girlfriend and then engage in whatever activity the parents had expressly refused to allow them to do. Then they would either sneak back to their own bedroom at home or stay at a friend's home for a short period. When staying at a friend's house, the girl would telephone her parents late at night or the next morning to explain what had happened and to ask to come home.

The four runaways characterized as Social Pleasure Seekers were away from home at least twenty-four hours. However, in the non-runaway sample, two girls could be classified as Social Pleasure Seekers. Both girls left home without parental permission to attend a particular social gathering but were absent for less than twenty-four hours. One girl was able to return home, her absence undetected by her parents. The parents of the other girl realized that their daughter was missing, located her whereabouts, and brought her home. Because neither girl was absent from home for twenty-four hours, they do not meet this study's definition of a runaway.

Depending upon the parents' reaction to the first runaway episode and the family's method of dealing with future conflict, runaway episodes may become more frequent, and the youth can be considered a Runaway Manipulator.

Level 2+ — Runaway Manipulators: For Runaway

Manipulators frequent conflict exists between parent and teenager over many facets of parental treatment. Four runaways experienced a similar pattern of on-going parental conflict mostly in the form of criticism and verbal arguments about the youngsters' attitudes, handling of responsibilities at home, and choice of friends. Runaway Manipulators perceive that siblings and friends are treated differently and better than they are treated. Runaway Manipulators run away in the hope that by leaving home temporarily, there will be a "cooling off" period during which parents will worry about them and accept them back on the teeenagers' own terms. In this study, the four Runaway Manipulators came from intact homes, and their grades in school were average or above. Shellow, et. al. (1967:29) also described the manipulative runaway:

> [The runaway act] may be a calculated maneuver in their dealings with parents, ultimately designed to change the relationship rather than to deny it.

Level 3+   Runaway Retreatists: Runaway Retreatists are based on the characteristics on twelve youths who impulsively ran from more intense conflict than that faced by Runaway Manipulators. Frequent arguments occurred with one or both parents yelling and occasionally hitting or throwing objects at the youth. Seven of the twelve Runaway Retreatists in this study were from broken homes. The overwhelming majority had one or more school problems; they had failed at least one course, had been suspended, or got left back. Runaway Retreatists exhibit escapist behavior by getting "wasted" on marijuana, or getting drunk on alcohol almost daily prior to running away.

Level 4+ — Endangered Runaways: The habitual conflicts between parents and Endangered Runaways result in these youths being the victims of repeated physical or sexual abuse inflicted on them by parents and step-parents, often while the parent was drunk. In this study, eight of the thirty runaways experienced the Level 4 intensity of conflict. Six of the eight had school problems. In most cases an alcoholic or ex-alcoholic parent was in the home. All Endangered Runaways regularly used amphetamines, LSD, cocaine or mescaline; half also had drinking problems. All eight were victims of recurring physical abuse, and two of those were also subjected to sexual abuse. When Endangered Runaways run away from home, it is often because of a beating that has recently occurred or the threat of yet another beating in retaliation for some real or imagined misbehavior.

In addition to reporting their successful use of coping mechanisms and minimal family conflict, the non-runaways revealed patterns of competence in the cognitive and affective domains.

ATTITUDE TOWARD SCHOOL

Although one-half of the runaway group seemed unable to view *any* aspect of school in a positive way, not one of the non-runaways gave such a response.

Thirteen of the runaways and fifteen of the non-runaways basically agreed that school was primarily a place for socializing with friends. However, nine of the non-runaways compared to only one runaway cited the opportunity to learn as the best aspect of school. Specific opinions of the non-runaways were:

"The best thing is learning,"
"Learning things I'm interested in,"
"Widening the field of learning,"
"Learning about different things — broadens your outlook,"
"Knowing that I'm learning makes me feel good,"
"Being able to choose what courses I want to take, for example more mathematics courses,"
"Future studies course, it is all about the future — future shock and things of the future."

When asked to identify the "worst" aspect of school, just over two-thirds (21) of the runaways mentioned homework or studying (7), school altogether (6), rules and regulations (5), and teachers (3). Of the thirty non-runaways, only three said they disliked homework and studying and four disliked their schedules or the requirement of getting to school early in the morning. More of the non-runaways (7) than the runaways (2) reported that they did not feel there was a "worst" part of school. Those non-runaways who did mention a "worst" feature of school were articulate in their response. The most frequent type of comment registered by the non-runaways was a specific concern about the content of classes. Their comments included:

> "Being in a class which does not help further my education,"
> "Classes that have no value,"
> "Too many tests in the same day,"
> "The pressure to do well and the monotony sometimes wears me down,"
> "There is a lot of competition for grades."

Almost all of the non-runaways had grade point averages from seventy five to ninety-five, with the mean at 85. In sharp contrast, most runaways had failed one or more courses during the previous school year, and their mean average for the past two years ranged between sixty-seven and seventy.

Not surprisingly, these findings seem to indicate that the non-runaways had considerably more positive feelings toward learning and school than did the runaways.

LEISURE-TIME ACTIVITIES

As reported, a large number of runaways and non-runaways experienced stress and crisis, although more of the runaways had experienced three or more stresses. However, the non-runaways seem to have had alternative leisure-time activities to lessen and counteract stress. The majority of the non-runaways, compared to only a small number of the runaways, reported involvement in many constructive inherently interpersonal activities like team sports. These activities promote shared responsibility and an understanding of the importance of getting along with others.

The data on the afterschool and weekend leisure-time activities of runaways and non-runaways indicated that almost all of the runaway and non-runaways enjoyed listening to music. Twenty-nine runaways and all thirty non-runaways indicated that they enjoy listening to music every day. Some non-runaways and some runaways played musical instruments, enjoyed watching television and participated in sports. However, the number of runaways who enjoyed these activities was smaller than the non-runaways. Fourteen non-runaways played a musical instrument in contrast to nine of the runaways; and seventeen of the non-runaways participated in individual and team sports compared to eight of the runaways. Unexpectedly, two-thirds of the runaways said they were *not* interested in watching television, and a few of them were vehement in their denunciation of it.

Differences between the two groups were very pronounced concerning their academically related interests. Six non-runaways enjoyed reading as a leisure-time activity, but only one runaway enjoyed reading. Fourteen non-runaways but only two runaways mentioned that they did homework or school work in their leisure-time.

The runaways reported frequent involvement in getting "wasted" or "stoned" (20 runaways), "hanging-out" (15), and partying (10); the non-runaways reported less involvement in getting "stoned" (2 respondents); "hanging-out" (2); and partying on weekends (4). A large number of the non-runaways did smoke marijuana regularly, but these data reflect the adolescents' perceptions of their most frequent kinds of leisure-time activity.

The non-runaways cited twenty-five specific leisure-time activities and hobbies that none of the runaways mentioned. Specific activities can be classified into these groups: 1. creative interests like creative writing, photography, dancing, acting, silversmithing, painting, and sculpture; 2. energetic pursuits like bicycling, karate, weightlifting, gymnastics, dating, cheerleading, walking and shopping, and 3. interests which require patience, organization, particular equipment, or skills like coin and stamp collecting, making miniature cars and fixing bicycles and cars. Consequently, the runaways again are seen as

performing leisure role expectations less adequately than those
who do not run.

FUTURE GOALS

The runaways and non-runaways were asked: "What do you
think you will be doing five years from now?" Among the
runaways, almost one-half (13) did not have a future goal;
however, only two of the non-runaways had no future goal. The
adolescents' future aspirations revealed that almost five times
as many of the non-runaways (24), compared to the runaways
(5), expected to prepare for their careers by attending college
and then, in several cases, going to graduate or law school.
These findings indicate an increased demonstration of
scholastic achievement by the non-runaways; a willingness by
the non-runaways to defer for several years the gratification of
earning money and being independent; and the non-runaways'
expected reliance on their parents for financial support during
college attendance.

The thirteen runaways who expressed no future goals gave
the following types of responses as to what they thought they
would be doing in five years;

I don't know. I can't look that far ahead.

— a sixteen-year-old boy.

Still partying and hanging out with my friends.

— a seventeen-year-old girl.

I probably be dead because no one wants me and I have no
place to go.

— a fifteen-year-old boy.

In school or dead.

— a seventeen-year-old girl.

The two non-runaways who reported no future goals commented:

> "I really don't know."
> "Beats the hell out of me."

Five of the non-runaways said they planned to do graduate work in law and business, but only one runaway expected to earn a bachelor's degree and enter medical school.

Seven runaways and three non-runaways expressed vocational goals, which did not require a bachelor's degree. Both groups seem generally interested in occupations which require some training after high school in a technical or other specialized program. The runaways were interested in becoming a legal secretary, cosmetologist, hair cutter in own shop, model, jockey, auto mechanic, and air conditioner repairman. The non-runaways were interested in becoming a police officer, hair cutter, and professional actor and dancer.

NON-RUNAWAYS WHO CONSIDERED RUNNING

How many teenagers thought about running away from home, but for some reason never actually did run? A large number (fourteen of the thirty) of the non-runaways said that they had thought about running away.

Shellow, et. al. (1967:27) reported that one-third of the 1,327 youths who answered a questionnaire in their public school sample had seriously considered running away but did not actually run. As a result, these researchers cautioned others "against making too much of clear-cut differences between those who run away and these who do not." In this study, information was collected pertaining to the reasons why the potential runaways did not leave home.

Seven of the fourteen non-runaways who had thought about running due to stressful events indicated that they did not leave because of the potential negative effects running away might have on their relationship with their parents. Consequently, some youths, in sharp contrast to the runaways, were able to realistically and logically assess the consequences of running away prior to undertaking actions. Their thought processes were illustrated in their statements:

> "I realized that it would not accomplish anything at all; in fact would make it worse,"
> "Running away doesn't solve anything, it just causes heartache for both parties,"
> "I thought of my parents,"
> "I would think about it and decide it was idiotic. I would say to myself, 'Where would you run to? You have a family who loves you. You have differences but they're basically good.' I saw friends who accomplished nothing by running away. One girl climbed out of a second floor window and broke her leg. Others went down the drain."

The other seven potential runaways gave different responses as to why they had not run away. Two made statements which implied they felt that running away took courage which they did not have. They "chickened out," and said, "I was chicken." Two were unclear about what happened and stated, "I just didn't" and "don't remember." Two others indicated that the stress abated or the conflict was resolved: "I just got over it," and "I went to my room and went to sleep and had forgot about it the next day." The other potential runaway viewed the controlling of her impulse to leave home as a challenge: "I tried to reason it out by myself. It was a challenge to see if I could handle it — myself and the problem."

These potential runaways displayed an ability to anticipate the negative consequences of impulsive, risk-taking behavior like running away and to control their desires for immediate gratification by engaging in alternative behavior; that ability is indicative of moral development.

VI. Parental Views and Perceptions

Most studies of adolescent runaways as well as juvenile delinquents do not evaluate the extent of agreement between adolescents' self-reported behavior and parents' perceptions. Particularly in a retrospective study, it is useful to have an additional source of data which provides a means of verifying the information obtained. Therefore, the goal was to interview as many of the parents of the thirty runaways and thirty non-runaways as possible. A subsample of ten parents of the runaways and twelve parents of the non-runaways was interviewed to provide additional information on the incident triggering a runaway episode, age, family structure, stressful events, and the type of discipline most frequently administered to the youngsters.

The runaways' parents were generally reluctant to be interviewed. Some of the runaways' parents were rarely home and when finally reached by telephone indicated that they were not interested in being interviewed. Eight of the interviews with parents of runaways were arranged following one to three telephone calls, and they usually were conducted in the parent's home. In the two other cases, parents said that they were too busy to be interviewed, one because of long working hours and the other because of holding two jobs. Interviews were eventually arranged with both of them — one at a father's home one evening, and the other with a mother in a make-shift office of a large furniture store while another salesperson worked for her. Eight of the interviews were with mothers and two were with fathers.

The results of the interviews with parents lend empirical support to the runaways' reports. An analysis of the recollections of each dyad — runaway and his or her parent — indicated complete congruence on the following: age, family composition, type of parental discipline, and stressful life events. An analysis of the recollections of triggering incidents of each dyad indicated congruence in seven of the dyads. Runaway-parent congruence on these factors was analyzed in terms of whether each parent's recollection indicated complete agreement or disagreement with his or her runaway's recollection. The number of times of runaway-parent agreement was totaled to form a parent-runaway congruence indicator on each of the above five variables.

Parents of non-runaways generally appeared to be more cooperative than parents of runaways. All twelve interviews of non-runaways' parents were with mothers. These non-runaway parents seemed more articulate and relaxed during the interview than the runaways' parents had been; three of the twelve parents expressed the judgment that when a youth runs away it is the parent's fault. Those three mothers proudly remarked that they knew where their children are at all times, because they, their neighbor, or another mother always serves as a "volunteer chauffeur" in transporting their children from place to place.

Congruence among each of the non-runaway-parent dyads was analyzed with regard to age, family structure, type of parental discipline, and recent stressful events in the adolescents' lives. This analysis indicated complete congruence for each of the twelve dyads on age and family structure; almost complete congruence on recollections of recent stressful events and only seven of the twelve dyads showing congruence on types of parental discipline.

Although congruence existed on the current structure of the adolescents' families, one girl reported that she was living with her natural mother and step-father but her mother indicated that both of her children had been adopted when they were infants. The girl may have neglected to mention her adoption because the woman is the only mother the girl has ever known and is thought of as her "natural" mother. The girl may have thought that her adoption was private information, or she may have thought that her adoption had no relevance to her current attitudes, skills, and behavior.

TRIGGERING INCIDENT: RUNAWAY-PARENT DYADS

The parents' recollections of the incident triggering their child's runaway episode were closely related to the respective youth's perception of the triggering incident. This study was primarily concerned with the individual's perceptions of stress and the related incidents which trigggered the runaway act. Therefore, whether the parent agreed with the child's reason for leaving home was not at issue; what was of concern was whether or not the parent and child recalled the same incident as triggering the youth's leaving home.

The findings indicate that congruence existed in seven of the ten runaway-parent dyads of the recollections of the incident triggering the first runaway episode. For example, one mother and daughter agreed about the conflict and tension leading to running away (congruence):

> Runaway: I was messing up in school, failing and cutting out, and getting high. She [her mother] grounded me. We argued about it [being grounded]. She said, "If you don't like my rules, leave. Go see if you can live with your father."

> Mother: I told her I hated kids and she should go live with her father. She learned that he could care less. Taking her

out once a week was more than enough for him.

A father and son disagreed about the triggering incident: (incongruence)

> Runaway: I didn't think my parents were treating me right. He doesn't like me going out at night, drinking, partying. He wants me to be a prisoner, to work around the house all the time and sit and talk to him every night.

> Father: He lies a lot. He keeps everything to himself. He does everything you ask him not to do — smoking pot, missing school, dressing like an animal, getting to school late, staying out late. . .

Another boy reported that when he had come home drunk, his mother began accusing him of responsibility for his father's death. Certain elements in the reports of the son and mother coincided; they both remembered the mother's locking the refrigerator door and becoming angry and throwing things at her son, but the boy said that his mother had repeatedly accused him of causing his father's death. The mother did not mention that she had made that accusation:

> Runaway: I came home drunk and she wouldn't let me have the key to the refrigerator. She was yelling and throwing things at me. She knew I was an alcoholic. My father died of alcoholism. She kept accusing me of my father's death.

> Mother: He's a destructive child and would lie like anything. . .He came in one night and he was stoned. He just stared at me like I was not even there. He stared right through me. He starts banging his fists on my refrigerator. He wants food and wants to watch my TV. He sees the sign in the kitchen, no food unless you clean my car. I'll never feed that kid again. . .I could see he wanted to go back out again. I says, "Oh, no." So I locked the door. So all he kept on doing was marching around here. So he

was just tormenting me. This is something Mike just loves to do. He loves to torment. So I said "No." So he go over through here and he go over and he unlocked the door. So I got mad and I start throwing stuff. And I don't care what anybody says. I will admit it. I even hit my husband one time. . . So he went out. He wasn't coming back here. So he was gone. I reported it to the police. I didn't want anything to come back to me saying I did something wrong. I went out immediately and reported it to the police.

The mother and son also gave different information about the cause of the father's death. Mike reported that his father was an alcoholic who died from cirrhosis of the liver; his mother said that her husband died of pneumonia and kidney failure. The mother finally admitted that her husband had been an alcoholic but she said that his drinking was under control when he died. Furthermore, Mike's mother felt that her son had not been remorseful enough about his father's death:

I called him at home and he cried. Mike cried for a few days and then thought it was a big party — was drinking and stoned all the time.

The mother and son's lack of communication and misunderstandings about the father's death are evident. Mike said that he was quite upset at his father's death and apparently dealt with his depression by retreating into drugs and alcohol. The mother misinterpreted his retreat as a sign that her son was partying and having a good time.

An indication of Mike's emotional problems in coping with his father's hospitalization and death became apparent by both mother and son saying that he felt he was a "jinx." According to the mother, one of her sisters was hospitalized for a heart condition and Mike's mother wanted him to visit his aunt. The mother recalls what her son's reaction was:

He tells me that he is a jinx. . .He doesn't want to go to the hospital. He is afraid if he is going to the hospital they will die. If he sees them, they will die. He visited my husband in the hospital and he died a day later. He saw my sister and she died. My brother-in-law died and he didn't see him.

The mother did not indicate that she had made any effort to allay her son's concerns. On the contrary, she seemed to have believed that her son may have been a jinx, by saying "What he wants is to hurt me. . .He's always been trouble for me."

PARENTAL DISCIPLINE: RUNAWAY-PARENT DYADS

Congruence between runaways and parents was indicated in all ten dyads concerning recollections on the type of parental discipline most frequently used.

A fifteen-year-old runaway said that she gets "yelled at, dragged to my room and slapped." The mother confirmed her daughter's statement:

> A couple of times my husband has lost his temper, maybe once a year, and given her a good spanking. She doesn't get beaten. It's just a spanking on her behind. Sometimes she'll get fresh and I'll slap her across the face. And we expect her to talk to us and she doesn't want to talk to us. I yell, my husband. . .sometimes he's had to drag her up [to her room] if she won't go. She wasn't an affectionate baby. She wasn't clingy.

A fourteen-year-old runaway indicated that he was disciplined by being yelled at and getting beaten. His father, an electrician, was unemployed for eight months. During that time, the father's alcohol problem became pronounced, and he beat his son more often when he was drunk. When asked about the type of discipline he used the father responded:

> If I was mad and I got upset, if I was short-tempered, he might have gotten it. Put it this way, he's not beaten all the time but he's gotten his beatings. He's been hit.

The son said he knew that if his father was not home for dinner, he would come home late at night, and his parents would start arguing. Sometimes his father would rush into his son's room and start beating him because his father did not like the kind of music his son was playing. Finally the boy ran away by climbing out of a bedroom window and hiding at a friend's house for several months.

In most other cases, the most frequent type of parental discipline was described almost word for word by the runaways and their parents. When the wording was not identical, the differences were due to the parents expounding in more detail than their children on the punishment used.

STRESSFUL EVENTS: RUNAWAY-PARENT DYADS

The runaway-parent dyads displayed complete congruence on their recollections of specific stressful events which had occurred in the lives of the runaways. It seemed to be particularly difficult for the parents of the runaways to recognize that stressful events which had affected the adults in the family had also affected the children. The only one stress — failures in school — was clearly recognized by parents as affecting the lives of youths.

Some runaways gave more detailed explanations than their parents of the situations leading to and surrounding a stressful event like their parents' divorce. In other cases, the parents elaborated in more detail than their children had on the occurrence of stressful experiences, in descriptions of an illness or surgical operation which they or their spouse had experienced or their becoming unemployed.

Stressful events of runaways can be understood by viewing the stress as perceived by the youth and the parent in the context of the family relationship.

Illustration of congruence: A seventeen-year-old girl was suddenly faced with her mother's illness and hospitalization. After the mother was discharged from the hospital, the girl began to perceive an over-protective attitude on the part of her mother. The mother seemed not to recognize that her daughter had suddenly been thrust into the role of "surrogate mother" during her mother's hospitalization. The daughter resented being treated like a child after she had been forced to handle and had faithfully performed adult responsibilities.

The mother had been hospitalized for three months with a bone disease. Because of the illness, the mother had to leave her job as a jewelry salesperson which she had always enjoyed. The woman experienced great stress both from the pain of osteomylitus and having to stay at home. She did say that her daughter was very good at that time, doing the cooking and taking care of her younger brother and sister. The mother felt that the experience was not stressful for the daughter but was merely a way to make her more responsible.

The daughter, Amy, said that she liked taking care of her brother and sister and that it was easy to cook for her father who usually worked late and would eat leftovers when he came home. On weekends her father would take the children to eat; then they would go to the hospital to visit the mother. Amy felt that she did not experience stress until her mother was discharged from the hospital. During the months that her mother was convalescing at home, she did not want Amy to date boys and was, Amy thought, very demanding about having a clean house. The girl smoked marijuana but said that her mother knew she was smoking and chose to ignore it. When police caught Amy and her friends smoking marijuana in a park near her home, major family arguments ensued. According to Amy:

> They wanted to put me in a hospital [an archaic state psychiatric hospital nearby]. They thought I was a crazy person. They kept me in the house. She had me grounded and took me everywhere she went.

Donna, a fifteen-year-old whose father is an ex-alcoholic and whose mother seems to be indifferent toward her reported:

> Anything I do is wrong. . .it's not just that I didn't do it the way she wanted me to, it's every time I do it, it's always wrong.

Donna said that when her mother became an active participant in Weight Watchers, the daughter felt ignored:

> Before she joined Weight Watchers, mother was very heavy and didn't care. . .now mother is too involved in W.W. activities.

Although Donna's father had been an alcoholic, Donna says that her mother had told her, "When [your] father gets better, everything else will get better." The father did overcome his drinking problem but the relationship between Donna and her mother only deteriorated further:

> He got better and my father and me, we're really close now but me and my mother, we've just. . .I don't even pay attention to her. I don't even talk to her anymore. I won't even say, "Hello," to her or "goodbye" or "good night" or "good morning." Most of the time, you start talking to her and she just like drifts off and then you sit there and you ask her a question and it's like sitting there talking to four walls.

Donna's father summarized the way he used to treat Donna and her three younger brothers and sisters when he was drinking:

> Total neglect. The only thing they were good for were gofers — go for a beer, get me this, get me that.

He felt that the current family problem was a lack of communication which was particularly evident between his wife and Donna:

> My wife does not take the time to talk to Donna. She is not only a daughter but a person.

Parents were asked what their reaction had been when they realized their children had run away. Reactions varied from anger to indifference to concern. Their recollections of their reaction were as follows:

> "Total surprise. Anger, pure and simple fury,"
> "I was absolutely irate,"
> "I figured she would leave,"
> "I expected it. He told me he was running away,"
> "It was a mutual thing. I threw her out,"
> "I felt useless,"
> "I was very apprehensive,"
> "I was scared for her sake. There were pimps following teenage girls in the city. I was frantic. We called the police and reported her missing.

PARENTAL DISCIPLINE: NON-RUNAWAY PARENT DYADS

Of all the factors studied, the lowest level of parent-youth congruence was found on the issue of discipline. There was congruence in seven of the twelve non-runaway-parent dyads' reports of the most frequent type of discipline. Two non-runaway adolescents and one parent either forgot or refrained from mentioning that hitting or slapping had been used as an occasional form of discipline; two youths either forgot or refrained from reporting a parent's punishment by means of threatening to or actually denying a privilege like the use of the telephone or being driven to a special event. These five instances of incongruence may have occurred because the slapping, grounding, or removal of privileges was done only rarely so that the youth or parent did not view them as the "most frequent" types of parental discipline. Also, concern over using guilt regarding administering discipline, especially corporal punishment may have been on the parents' minds more than on the youths' minds.

Illustrations of congruence: A fifteen-year-old girl indicated that her parents yell at her and that they used to hit or slap her occasionally when she was being punished. Her mother agreed.

> I scream, yell, rant. My husband is in a very stressful business [carpet store, a family business]. He tends to ex-

plode more often. She used to get hit when she was younger. I rapped her in the rear about a month ago and she said, "I am fifteen years old and you shouldn't do that to me."

A fifteen-year-old boy said that his step-father told him he watches too much television and set a limit on the amount of time he can watch. Congruence was shown when the youth's mother stated that when her son was not getting above a ninety grade in all of his subjects, punishment was "no TV after a certain hour."

A sixteen-year-old girl indicated that her parents are lenient with her and that they discuss problems with her. The mother remarked that when a potential problem arises like her daughter wanting an extended curfew, "She'll say it's a big party. I need to stay out til 2:00. We'll compromise."

Illustrations of incongruence: A fifteen-year-old boy indicated that his mother disciplined him by scolding and yelling. The mother indicated that she does yell but she also denies privileges. She had been annoyed by her son's long hair and uncut long toenails, and because her son is an avid coin collector, she threatened to remove a privilege. She told him:

> I'll take you to the coin show [which was about twelve miles away with no public transportation available] if you cut your toenails.

Although angered by his mother's insistence on his cutting his toenails, he did oblige her because he wanted to attend the coin show.

A sixteen-year-old girl reported that her parents discipline her by scolding, yelling or by sending her to her room. Her mother, however, reported the following kinds of discipline:

> Yelling, denial of privileges, such as not being allowed to use the telephone, and occasional hitting or slapping.

Another sixteen-year-old girl said that her mother scolded,

criticized, and yelled at her. In contrast, the mother revealed that, in addition to yelling and criticizing, she also grounds her daughter and denies privileges. When the girl brought home a failure notice for the first time in mathematics — an early warning of failing at midterm — the mother reported:

> I didn't let her go out during the week [evenings]. Other times she was given only part of her allowance.

STRESSFUL EVENTS: NON-RUNAWAY-PARENT DYADS

There was congruence in eleven of the twelve non-runaway-parent dyads regarding their recollections of stressful events in the adolescents' recent past. Steve was the only example of incongruence.

A fifteen-year-old boy reported having experienced no stressful events. His mother, however, discussed an event which she felt had been quite stressful for her son. A year before when in the ninth grade, the boy received a two-day suspension from school for possessing a small amount of marijuana. The mother recounted the following course of events:

> Steve was suspended for two days because he bought pot from a kid acoss the street. Other kids were also caught with pot in school. The school handled it the wrong way. Everyone in school knew. He went back to school after the suspension and spoke to each teacher at the end of class and told them he is the same person, the same good student and is willing to discuss this. His teachers were very understanding. They told him that they know he is still the same hardworking person and when they were young they also did some foolish things. The principal had called the police station and I had to go to the police [juvenile officer] and pick Steve up. My husband was called at work. He came home in a rage — broke Steve's records. I was very upset but explained that we would stick by him, that he is our son and this should be a learning experience not to get

involved with pot.

Among the eleven cases illustrating congruence, a sixteen-year old non-runaway girl reported three heavy stresses: moving to a smaller house in the next town; the aftermath of bankruptcy of her father's business and a broken romance. The girl's recollections were as follows:

> My father's business went bankrupt. We had threatening people come to the house. He [her father] was in a depression. My mother got a job and was supporting us. One guy came in the back way [at the back entrance to the house and started a fight [with her father]. It was frightening. . .I came to certain realizations about myself that led me to break off a relationship I had with a boy. I was living under the illusion that I was satisfied. Then I realized our relationship was based on nothing but dreams. We were living a fantasy and I was fooling myself and him, and had to end it. After. that I went into a depression. I lacked self-respect, I was disappointed that my ideals couldn't be lived up to. I truly wanted our relationship to be special but I could not go on pretending. . .I hurt him incredibly. I felt so guilty. . .Our relations were always apart from anything real, like my family. I never discussed it with anyone in my family.

The girl's mother said that her husband had been unemployed for a year-and-a-half because of bankruptcy. Lack of the father's income necessitated their moving to a smaller house and her getting a job. The mother seemed embarrassed about the situation and did not want to elaborate. She was unaware of her daughter's broken romance; however, that she did not know about the broken romance did not affect the congruence of their dyad, because the daughter had clearly said that she had told no one in her family about it.

In three examples of congruence, the parents of non-runaways elaborated in much greater detail than their children about the nature of a serious illness of a family member.

Mrs. A. talked about a back operation which her non-runaway son had had two years ago, requiring a ten-day hospital stay. When the youth's back "went in spasm," she immediately contacted the boy's uncle, an orthopedic specialist, who met them at the hospital. The youth's back problem was diagnosed as osteoplastomy — lesion in the bone. Following the surgery, Mrs. A. reported that her son was much improved. She mentioned that a further cause of anxiety had been the possibility that he would have to wear a brace but the brace was not necessary.

In the interviews with Mrs. B. and Mrs. C., the mothers discussed: the nature of a non-runaway boy's step-sister's illness, Von Hipples Landau Syndrome, a disorder of the central nervous system, and a mother's colitis condition. In the above descriptive cases, the elements of the stresses were congruent in each of the dyads.

VII. Runaway Experiences

The suburban runaways were running to places close to their homes. Of the thirty runaways, twenty-two went to places within a radius of ten miles from their homes; fourteen went to a friend's house; six went to a local site like a park or school; and two went to relatives' homes in the same town. Bonee, reporting on runaways in Massachusetts, noted that the majority of runaway youths "often choose to remain in their own communities among friends" rather than going out-of-state (Bonee, 1974:360). Shellow, et. al. (1967:14) reported that in three-quarters of their Montgomery County sample, runaways "never got beyond the metropolitan area" of Washington, D.C.

Only eight of the suburban runaways fled to New York City or out-of-state. Of those, four planned to go to Florida, and a fifth hoped to reach Missouri, her former home state. While hitchhiking in either New Jersey or Delaware, all five were intercepted by police. That only three of the runaways wanted to go to New York City might be surprising, considering the fact that New York City has been receiving much publicity as a destination for runaways from across the country. However, the small number of youths fleeing to Manhattan may be explained by the fact that these youths, living on Long Island which is part of the New York metropolitan area, in all likelihood were familiar with the big city. Therefore, New York City may not have had the "magical" appeal which it might hold for someone from a city which is further away and not as accessible as New York had been to the youths in this sample.

There does not seem to be a relationship between the amount of stress in the lives of the runaways and their having fled to a local versus a distant destination. There were almost an equal number of local runaways experiencing three or more stresses as there were non-local runaways under heavy stress, and amount of stress did not seem to influence the runaways' choice of destination.

Most of the respondents' descriptions of their runaway experiences reflect their desire to find refuge close to home:

— I talked to Joe and his parents said I could stay there.

— a seventeen-year-old boy.

— I left at 2:30 in the morning and went to a few friends' houses. He [her abusive father] was out looking for me and found me Sunday night.

— a fourteen-year-old girl.

— I hitched down the road to my friend's house.

— a sixteen-year-old boy.

— Slept in his car [the abusive father's car, in the parking lot next to their apartment building.

— a fifteen-year-old boy.

— My cousin found me under the bleachers at the high school.

— a sixteen-year-old girl.

PERSONS WHO WERE HELPFUL TO RUNAWAYS

The runaways considered one or two friends, more than any other people, to have been helpful during the runaway episode. Reliance upon the assistance of a friend occurred in more than half (17) of the cases. Friends aided the runaways by sharing their bedroom or providing a finished basement, a backyard or their parents' car as shelter. Friends also provided food and companionship to the runaways. The living conditions at friends' houses varied considerably depending upon whether or not the friend's parents knew that the runaway was staying at their house. In the twelve cases in which the friend's parents knew about the situation, the runaway openly became an accepted addition to the friend's family. Runaways ate meals with the rest of the family and had free access to the house. One friend and her mother kept the runaway's presence a secret from the father, and the youth had freedom to move around the house only when the father was not at home. Dinner was smuggled to the runaway when the father had finished eating in the kitchen and had left for the den. The most difficult and uncomfortable living situations occurred for four runaways each aided by a friend who did not want the parents to know what was happening, for fear that the parents would immediately notify the runaway's parents. Whenever either of the parents was at home, the runaway was confined to a "hiding place" in cramped quarters like a garage, backyard, or basement. Undetected, the runaway ate only what the friend could smuggle from the kitchen and what would not be noticed as missing by other family members. The meager food supply was supplemented at times with food which the runaway shoplifted from a local foodstore on brief outings during the day.

Five runaways turned to a relative for food and shelter. Three turned to a cousin, one to an aunt, and one to an older sister who had a home of her own. Five runaways reported that they had been helped by a truck driver, guidance counselor, or strangers, and they usually received direct or indirect aid in the form of transportation or shelter. Five youths stated that no one was particularly helpful to them during the runaway episode — they

felt that they had survived completely on their own. One girl
commented that she was grateful to the police for taking her to a
hospital. She had been on a "bad trip" and was acting "violent-
ly," refusing to give the police her name or any identifying information.

PERSONS PERCEIVED AS HARMFUL BY RUNAWAYS

Because twenty-two runaways were provided with a place to
sleep and food by either a close friend or relative, it is not surprising that only six of the runaways felt that someone had been
harmful to them while on the run.

These youths expressed anger toward people they felt had
jeopardized their flight — an uncle, sibling, friend or police officer. These people had reported where the runaway was staying
and prompted the youth's subsequent return home. Two youths
complained about the conditions to which they were subjected
while being detained by police. Diane recalled how she and her
girlfriend had been treated: "We got picked up by the cops in
New Jersey — troopers." After approximately six hours in
police custody, the parents of Diane's friend arrived and took
them both home. While they were waiting, the girls were confined to a jail cell; according to Diane:

> The state trooper locked us in the cement cell. Cement ben-
> ches, toilet, sink. It was ice cold in there and we were so
> tired. We couldn't sleep on the benches because they were
> so hard.

PROBLEMS ENCOUNTERED BY RUNAWAYS

What problems do youths experience while on the run and as a
result of their parents' punitive reactions? Generally, the
youths reported having had problems meeting basic needs for
shelter, food, and clothing. None reported having been molested
or assaulted. Six runaways reported that they had no money;
eight reported having had police problems; four said they did
not have enough food; and three could not find a place to sleep.

Seventeen-year-old Maryann reflected on her experience, including a police threat that she would be put into the overcrowded, understaffed New York City Detention Center which was widely known to be a deplorable place:

> I ran with my girlfriend, Kathy, to the city. . .We took a train. On Sunday me and Kathy were on mescaline and had three hits. We were hanging out on 48th Street. I had a beer in my hand and we had joints. The police asked us for I.D. Kathy got snotty. She started screaming and cursing the cops because she was fifteen and knew they couldn't do anything to her. . .They took us to the station for loitering and running away. . .Kathy's parents picked her up and said it was all my fault and yelled at me. The cops were going to put me in Spofford Detention Center. They said I would probably get gang raped there and become real ugly after the rats got to me. . . My uncle is a cop in the city. He got me out of there. He spoke to the police and took me home.

Doug reported being handcuffed by the police for six-and-a-half hours to the floor of a small detention room near Newark, New Jersey:

> I tried to get to Florida. Didn't make it. The state troopers got us for hitchhiking. Cops handcuffed all of us and brought us to the police station. It was uncomfortable being handcuffed to the floor from 3:30 to 10:00 — not knowing when my father would pick me up.

On the second and last time she had run away, Judy was gone for six weeks. Her father signed a PINS petition resulting in her incarceration in the Children's Shelter for four days.

> It was like a tomb — all gray. Ceiling gray, floor gray. There was a bed, one blanket, and a metal desk in the corner. I was thinking of slashing my wrists on it. I had a strep throat. . . overflowing toilet. I imagined an elf was under the bed.

Barbara, age fifteen, and her friend had difficulty getting food while on the run. They approached a boy who was eleven or twelve years old, "just hanging out" in a school yard, and according to Barbara:

> I asked some kid if he could go to his house and get me something to eat and I said even if it's a piece of bread, I don't care. So the little kid went to the store and he bought us a loaf of bread and a box of donuts each.

Betty, a sixteen-year-old, had been sleeping in her girlfriend's back yard for three months. Her main problem seemed to be getting food. She reported matter-of-factly that she had resorted to stealing most of her food from a local supermarket.

VIII. Conclusion

An examination of the stressful events in the lives of runaways provides a conceptual means for understanding the runaway phenomenon. The data revealed that stressful events had a major influence on the lives of the adolescents studied. It was found that stress is more likely to occur among runaways than among non-runaways and that specific patterns of daily living were apparent among the runaways and seemed to contribute to their running away.

A way of conceptualizing runaways by means of a parent-youth conflict continuum was presented. It was postulated that there are several analytic types of runaways, and each type has a unique set of characteristics which distinguishes it from the others. Four types of parent-youth conflict apparently preceded runaway acts. Youths of one type — comprised of Runaway Explorers and Pleasure Seekers — encountered minimal conflict with their parents. The primary areas of conflict and friction arose from a single issue which a youth felt to be of particular importance, like the imposition of an early curfew. Problems experienced by another type — Runaway Manipulators — were characterized by frequent conflict with parents over many kinds of parental behavior. The source of the conflict for Manipulators may have also been the result of differing opinions about the youth's attitudes, behavior, and choice of friends. Manipulators used the runaway act as a way of getting their parents to relent on issues about which there had been arguments. A third type of adolescent — Runaway Retreatists — experienced intense situations of conflict and tension. Arguments were accompanied by a parent's hitting, slapping, or throwing objects at a youth. Retreatists resorted to getting "high" on drugs or intoxicated on alcoholic beverages almost daily prior to running away. Finally, a fourth type of youngster — Endangered Runaways — experienced habitual conflicts in which repeated physical and/or sexual abuse was inflicted upon them by a parent or step-parent. These runaways fled to escape the physical peril within their home situations.

This study identified four primary explanations for the runaway phenomenon:

1. Running away is a response to experiencing three or more stressful events. The runaway interview data indicated that in most cases, three or more recent stressful events were reported by adolescents.

2. Running away occurs when adolescents experience stressful events and are unsuccessful in reducing the stress with traditional coping methods. Many of the non-runaways sought the assistance of a parent or relative when trying to resolve a difficult problem. However, most runaways not only did not seek the assistance of their parents but often blamed them as the source of the stress. The absence or presence of significant other people seemed important in explaining runaway phenomena. Finally, most runaways reported the use of negative coping methods like taking drugs or drinking alcohol.

3. Stress is experienced to a greater extent in the lives of the runaways than in the lives of the non-runaways. A total of 130 (an average of 4.33) stressful events were experienced by the thirty runaways during the four-year period preceding the interviews. In contrast, the thirty non-runaways experienced a total of only 76 (an average of 2.53) stressful events during the same four-year period.

4. Runaways in crisis do not have patterns of competence to reduce the impact of their crises. Patterns of competence can be seen by examining the cognitive and affective skills an adolescent demonstrates in school and in leisure-time activities. Nonrunaways characteristically express positive attitudes toward school and rarely fail courses. They also frequently participate in specific constructive leisure-time activities like basketball, baseball, and tennis. However, runaways often express negative attitudes toward school, do poorly in classes, and spend their leisure-time getting "wasted" or "stoned."

LEGAL ISSUES AFFECTING RUNAWAYS

Throughout the United States, the traditional method of dealing with runaways was incarceration. Runaways, along with truant and incorrigible youths, constitute a category known today as status offenders. Status offenses, as distinct from juvenile delinquency offenses, are defined as acts which are illegal *only* when committed by a juvenile.

It was not until the 1960's that individual state legislatures began to modify the juvenile code to separate status offenses from other juvenile delinquency offenses. New York State was a leader in this regard with its "persons in need of supervision" (PINS) legislation which was enacted in 1962. Since that time, many other states have adopted similar legislation.

The legislative acts in various states concerning status offenders have developed for these juveniles a terminology which varies somewhat from state to state. The terminology is easily identifiable by the acronym used in referring to these youths. The first word of the phrase may be "persons," "juveniles," "minors," or "children," but the last four words are generally the same — "in need of supervision." The resulting tag words become PINS, JINS, MINS, and CINS.

In some states, juvenile codes remain unchanged, and a runaway youth who is awaiting a court appearance can legally be detained in jail. In some small towns or in cities which have overcrowded facilities, runaways who are awaiting juvenile court disposition can be detained in a jail populated with adult offenders. After adjudications, some youths are still being sent to antiquated juvenile reformatories for a year or more.

In states where PINS legislation has been enacted for status offenders in need of supervision, mere passage of the legislation has been no solution for many existing problems. When PINS are recognized as a separate legal category from juvenile delinquents, there is growing recognition that the policy of demanding that PINS become involved in the court process is wrong, because it may be harmful to the youth and because PINS cases unnecessarily burden court backlogs. When a runaway youth commits an act which society may perceive as socially or morally wrong but which is not criminal, legally labelling a runaway youth as a PINS has become as much of a stigma for runaways as the previous label of "juvenile delinquent."

In most cases the passage of laws by state legislatures removed juvenile delinquency sanctions from status offenses and replaced incarceration with help from social service agencies. Not only have social services for PINS been inadequate but several studies conducted between 1972 and 1975 (Sarri, 1974; Cohen, 1975; New York State Council of Voluntary Child Care Agencies, 1975) have given evidence that status offenders sometimes received more severe penalties than juvenile delinquents. In many instances, runaway youths who have been convicted for juvenile delinquency offenses.

A youth who has fled from home following a beating by an alcoholic step-father while the youth's mother "looked the other way" needs a supportive therapeutic environment. It would be totally devastating to incarcerate such an adolescent even for a short period of time. Runaways who are labeled as status offenders are as PINS burdened with a juvenile court record. They are remanded to the same kinds of juvenile institutions as are youths who have been convicted of crimes like auto theft, assault, and robbery *unless* state law clearly specifies that status offenders may not be housed with juvenile delinquents. The debilitating effects of the incarceration of non-criminal youths have been well documented. It is necessary that alternatives to incarceration be provided for youthful status offenders who clearly need social services and placement in community group homes.

If, as this study indicates, a large number of runaways are in crisis and incarceration only exacerbates crisis, then community-based programs need to be implemented to provide these youths with crisis intervention, food, shelter, medical services, and appropriate referral services. Some emergency services and shelters are available for runaways, but long waiting lists to several group homes in the area of "Runaway Retreat" and elsewhere indicate a need to develop additional resources and adequate volunteer homes for runaways.

Three kinds of social services should be available to runaways and their families throughout the country. These services need to be planned and implemented in a way which will enable runaways in crisis to receive timely intervention.

1. While on the run, youths often need to find a drop-in center or runaway shelter where food, shelter, and counselling services are provided on an emergency 24-hour-a-day basis. Federal funding is presently available for shelters. These services should be publicized through public education programs to acquaint youths, their families, and professionals with the availability and nature of ther services. Collaborative interagency referral should also be encouraged from those who come in contact with runaways — police officers, school social workers, teachers, guidance counselors, probation officers, juvenile court judges, and hospital emergency room personnel.

2. After returning home, runaway youths with their parents may need the assistance of a social service agency which provides on-going individual, group, and family therapy.

3. When youths should not continue living with their families or relatives, a social service agency can try to provide an alternative living arrangement with foster parents, a therapeutically-oriented group home, or a residential treatment center where psychiatric and social services are provided.

SHORT- AND LONG-TERM PROGRAMS

Short-term programs should be operated 24-hours-a-day to meet the runaways' basic need for food and shelter and to provide crisis intervention, medical services, individual, group and family counseling services and referrals. Short-term programs are known by a variety of names including "crash pads," runaway shelters, and volunteer homes.

When a runaway youth comes to a short-term program, the youth worker should as a legal obligation notify the parents.

Depending upon the parent's wishes and the state law, the youth may be scheduled for a court appearance to be adjudicated as a "person in need of supervision." Initial casework and family counseling sessions should focus on reuniting the family which for many runaway cases is a realistic and workable goal of treatment. However, in conflict-ridden cases, when a youth refuses to return home or when the parents refuse to take the youth back, an alternative living situation must be found.

The most common long-term living arrangements seem to be foster family care and group care homes. In foster care, traditionally one or at most two youths were placed with foster "surrogate" parents. If social work, educational, or psychiatric services were considered necessary, they were obtained within the community. However, traditional foster care often provided "low board rates and inadequate casework supervision," which led to a decrease of good foster homes and a perpetuation of "low-quality foster family care" (Gula, 1964: 2-3). As a result, group foster homes of specialized foster homes came into existence. Foster parents, living in their own home, received a reasonable board rate for accepting between four to six "problem" youths who needed more support services than those which were generally available in a regular foster care situation.

About the same time that group foster care came into vogue, group care homes were evolving into small, personalized residential institutions with an emphasis on therapeutic community. Individual, group, and family therapy by professional social workers and psychologists was considered fundamental in group home programs. It is, however, difficult to generalize about the quality of services available at either specialized foster or group homes, because the quality of treatment varies from program to program. Furthermore, the terminology can be misleading, because the purpose and function of specialized foster homes and group homes can overlap. Generally, there seem to be three distinguishing factors between the two kinds of homes: 1. the number of youths who are in residence at any one time; 2. whether the adults in charge live in their own home where the youths are brought, or whether a governmental or private agency supervises the facility and hires adults to live and work there; and 3. the degree of monitoring and type of licensing which the local and/or state governments administer.

A group home can provide a viable long-term living arrangement for runaway youths. A group home usually has between seven and twelve youths in residence (Gula, 1973:14), living in one large house or in a series of adjacent apartments. The "houseparents," sometimes referred to as youth workers or child care workers, are augmented by professional staff who are available full-time or part-time and who are usually available in . case of an emergency. Scarcity of funds is a major problem for group home directors, as funding levels have a direct impact upon the quality of care provided to the runaways and other youths referred to a group home. Funding also affects how specialized the admission process and resulting services can be — will services be provided to a small number of youths with homogeneous problems or to a large number of youths with heterogeneous problems?

Because runaway youths have a history of running away from problems with which they cannot cope, foster parents and group home directors may be reluctant to accept adolescents who may run away from their facility. In areas where resources are particularly scarce, sometimes the only facility which will accept a runaway is a locked institution which by its very nature makes running away difficult. At a locked facility, runaway behavior is brought under control through custody; unless therapeutic intervention is provided, the problems which led the youth to run away will likely persist. Perhaps group homes could be developed specifically for runaways, with a professional staff on the premises who understood and could deal with runaway behavior. Staff members could be on-duty 24-hours-a-day so that middle of the night runaway attempts could be met with immediate crisis intervention counseling.

The findings of this study indicate a need for training additional family therapists to help youths cope with crisis situations and to develop ways to teach youths appropriate coping skills. The full range of social services should be made available to families of runaways. Most of the youths in this study fled home when the home situation became so stressful that it could no longer be tolerated. Social workers possess the training and experience to help families resolve their problems either through direct intervention or through referrals to practitioners who specialize in one particular treatment like family therapy, child abuse service, or vocational evaluation, training, and placement. When individual family members are referred to specialized treatment programs, the social worker should coordinate the various aspects of the entire treatment plan.

Finally, local hotline and drop-in services should be available seven days-a-week, including evenings so that adolescents who are living with their parents and are experiencing stresses may call or visit a social worker without making an appointment. An agency which is open only during the day or is even open one or two evenings a week does not provide adequate services for youths under stress.

FURTHER RESEARCH

Longitudinal research with large samples needs to be planned to determine whether a casual relationship exists between experiencing stress and running away from home. These studies should be conducted over a period of several years, allowing for the reinterviewing of the same people. Taking into account a longitudinal study's potential for violating juveniles' rights to privacy, one should carefully consider the ethical and legal issues of conducting follow-up interviews on a sample of cohorts, and proceed only when it is ethical and feasible to do so.

Future studies would help to determine the short-term and long-term effects of stressful events upon running away. They might also be useful in measuring differences between teenage runaways who experienced stress prior to and within two years after running away and those runaways who did not experience further crises.

It is recommended that future researchers investigate the following:

1. When chronic runaway acts occur frequently among youths from non-intact families, is the precipitant the broken home itself, the family conflict resulting from the break, or interacting factors?

2. Are there differences in the nature and number of recent stressful events according to race, religion, socioeconomic class, size of family, sibling ordinality, population density of residential area, personality type, or level of self-concept of runaways?

3. Will those adolescents who reported that they ran away because of being treated unfairly at home be more likely to be competent later in their adult lives than those who ran from physically or sexually abusive parents? "Competence" is defined as living independently of their parents, and working steadily three, five and ten years later.

4. Will the non-runaways lead more competent and independent lives than the runaways three, five, and ten years later?

5. Will those adolescents who are living with an alcoholic parent in an intact home be more likely to run away than those who are living with an alcoholic parent in a nonintact home?

6. After parents separate what types of stressful events occur to increase the likelihood of adolescents running away?

7. Will those who ran away once and then went to a counseling center of their own volition run away again?

8. Will those adolescents who had run away more than once run away again one year after having come to a counseling center?

9. Under what family situations and circumstances will first time runaways and repeaters be more likely to cease rather than continue their runaway episodes?

10. Do runaways perceive their parents' discipline toward them as more punitive than non-runaways?

11. How important a role does parental communication and attitude play in the formation of runaway behavior?

12. When a youth perceives parental figures as failing to be supportive and preoccupied with other activities, is the probability of the youth's engaging in runaway behavior significantly increased?

13. How important a role does adolescent heterosexual experience play in precipitating runaway behavior?

Not all youths respond to intense stress and frustration by failing in school, taking drugs and alcohol, becoming truant, and running away. Some seek the help and support of parents, siblings, or significant others. Some make a concerted effort to deal with stress through constructive coping mechanisms such as talking to parents, teachers, and counselors and channeling their frustrations and aggression into academic pursuits or hobbies.

The adolescent's response to stressful events depends on the youth's personality, an ability to use positive coping skills, and the response of parents and teachers to the youth. This study has provided evidence that some youths learn to overcome the stress and obstacles they encounter early in life by positive and growth-enhancing means. Others seek refuge in drugs and alcohol, while others resort to acting-out by exhibiting antisocial and delinquent behavior.

Renewed efforts should be directed toward primary prevention by encouraging the following: 1. involvement by educators and parents in child-rearing, parent education, and family life education courses; 2. encouraging the development of a relationship with one or more "significant others," so that turbulent feelings can be discussed freely and without fear of reprimand or punishment. Idealy a parent serves as a significant other but if this is not possible, the role can be filled by another trusted advisor, usually someone who is a little older and more experienced like a grandparent, aunt or uncle, cousin, older brother or sister, counselor or clergyman. Adolescence is a time characterized by upheaval and turmoil as a youth matures from childhood to adulthood. The strong foundation of a trusting relationship can be laid in the early years, the adolescent can learn to feel confident that his or her problems can be discussed freely: 3. involving children and youth in individual sports like swimming, weight lifting, gymnastics, bicycling and group sports like baseball, basketball, football, volleyball. 4. encouraging the expression of both happy and unpleasant emotions through involvement in the creative arts: writing poetry, keeping a diary, playing a musical instrument, participating in school or community dramatic groups, or developing an interest in drawing, painting, and sculpture.

Each youth needs to be accepted as a unique individual by parents, teachers, counselors, and neighbors. Each youth needs to be encouraged to set and reach positive goals at an individual pace. Each youth has a remarkable degree of untapped potential. Whether or not the self-actualization and well-being of today's youth become a dream of reality depends on the responsiveness of concerned adults.

Appendix I: Youth Interview Guide

First name: Number:

Location of Interview: Interview Date:

Opening Statement Made by Interviewer
    I want you to know that anything you say to me will be confidential. I do not need to know your full name or your address. Your real name won't be used in my study. I would like to learn as much as possible about runaways and non-runaways. It is important for me to learn about the daily activities, stressful experiences, attitudes and feelings of youths. To do this study, I need your help. I am going to ask you a number of questions. If you do not feel comfortable with any of the questions, you do not have to answer.
    There are no "right or "wrong" answers to any of the questions I am going to ask you. The best answers are the ones which describe the way you really feel about things.
    We're almost ready to start. But before we begin, do you have any questions or concerns about the interview? [I allowed time

for any questions the interviewee might have.]
Okay, let's begin.

1 . Do you enjoy music?
[If yes] do you enjoy listening to music?
Do you play a musical instrument?
[If yes] which musical instrument?

2 . Do you have any hobbies?
[If yes] what are they?
Approximately how much time do you spend each week on your hobby(ies)?

3 . Are you interested in sports?
[If yes] which sports do you like the best?
Approximately how much time do you spend each week watching or participating in sports?

4 . Do you enjoy watching television?
[If yes] what are three of your favorite TV shows?
Approximately how much time do you spend each night watching TV?

5 . How old are you?

6 . Who is living in your home? [With runaways who were living at Runaway Retreat's group home, the question was: Who was living in your home when you ran away?]

natural mother
step-mother
foster mother
grandmother
natural father
step-father
foster father
grandfather
sister(s) How many?
step-sister(s) How many?
brother(s) How many?

step-brother(s) How many?
aunt
uncle
cousin
boarder(s)
friend(s)
other

7 . [If the youth was not living with both natural parents] Did your parents break up because of divorce, separation, mother died, or father died?

8 . [If the youth's parents were not living together] Have either of your parents remarried? [If yes] how many times?

9 . Have you moved in the past five years? [If yes] what cities or counties have you lived in and for how long, starting with where you live now and working back.

10. What is the best thing about being in school?

11. What is the worst thing about being in school?

12. How are your doing in school?

13. Have you been unhappy or disappointed about something that happened in the past year? [If yes] what happened?

14. [If applicable] has your disappointment affected your school work? Please explain.

15. [If applicable] has your disappointment affected your family relations? Please explain.

16. [If applicable] has your disappointment affected the way you feel about yourself? Please explain.

17. During the past four years, have you experienced any stressful situations?
    [If yes] what happened?

18. When you have a heavy problem or crisis situation, is there any way that you can help yourself?
    [If yes] in what ways can you help yourself?

19. Is there anyone you can talk to when you have a problem?
    [If yes] what is their relationship to you?

20. Who in your home is working and what kind of work are they doing?

21. If your mother, father, [or guardian] is out of work, please tell me who is out of work and for approximately how long.

22. Do you think that your family understands you?
    [If not] please sum up what the problem(s) seem(s) to be.

23. Have either or both of your parents been suffering from a serious illness?
    [If yes] what illness and for how long?

24. Have you been hospitalized because of a serious illness?
    [If yes] what illness and for how long?

25. Do either [or both] of your parents drink excessively?
    [If yes] does your mother/father treat you differently when she/he has been drinking?
    [If applicable] how does she/he treat you differently?

26. Do your parents discipline you?
    [If yes I stated that parents use different types of discipline and asked] which type of discipline is used most frequently by your parents?

27. Have any of your friends ever run away from home?
    [If yes] do you know the reason why they left home?

[If yes] what was the reason?
[If applicable] how many of your friends have run away?

28. Have you ever run away from home?
    [If yes] how many times?

29. [If no to question number 28] have you ever thought about running away from home?
    [If yes] what were the reasons?
    [If applciable] what happened so that you didn't have to run away?

[The following questions were asked only if the youth had run away from home. If the youth indicated having had more than one runaway episode, these questions were asked of each act.]

30. What do you feel was the "last straw" that triggered your leaving home?

31. Please describe the events which led to your running away.

32. Before you ran away did you talk to anyone about it?
    [If yes] who did you talk to?

33. Did you have any problems after you ran away?
    [If yes] what problems did you have?

    money problems
    no place to sleep
    not enough food
    police problems
    other

34. Please describe what happened.

35. Do you feel that anyone was helpful to you while you were away from home?
    [If yes] who was helpful? Please describe.

friend
relative (what relation?)
teacher
clergyman
youth worker
police officer
other

36. Do you feel that anyone was harmful to you while you were
    away from home?
    [If yes] who was harmful? Please describe.

    friend
    relative (what relation?)
    teacher
    clergyman
    police officer
    youth worker
    other

37. Have you used any of the following drugs, and if so, what
    is the frequency of use?

    beer
    liquor
    marijuana
    THC
    LSD (acid)
    "uppers"
    "downers"
    cocaine
    heroin
    other

38. What do you think you'll be doing five years from now?

39. Do you have any additional comments?

Appendix II: Parent Interview Guide

1 . Who is living in your home?

2 . What is your marital status?

3 . How many times have you been married?

4 . Have you moved in the past five years?
[If yes] what cities or counties have you lived in and for how long, starting with where you live now and working back.

5. Who in your home is working and what kind of work are they doing?

6 . If anyone in your home (including yourself) has been unemployed, please specify who is or has been out-of-work, and for approximately how long.

7 . Have you or your spouse been hospitalized because of a serious illness?
[If yes] what illnsess and for how long?

8 . Have any of your children been suffering from a serious illness?
[If yes] what illness and for how long?

9 . Does anyone in your home drink excessively?
[If yes] do they act differently when they have been drinking?
[If yes] in what way?

10. Parents use different types of discipline with their children. Sometimes the mother is the disciplinarian; in other familes the father is the disciplinarian. Who is the disciplinarian in your home? What type of discipline is used most frequently?

11. Has your son/daughter ever run away from home?
[If yes] please describe the events that seem to have led up to your son/daughter's running away.
How did you feel after you realized that your son/daughter was gone?

References

Aguilera, Donna C. and Messick, Janice M. *Crisis Intervention: Theory and Methodology.* St. Louis: Mosby Co., 1974.

Aichorn, A. *Wayward Youth.* New York: Viking Press, 1935.

Ambrosino, Lillian. *Runaways.* Boston: Beacon Press, 1971.

Armstrong, Clairette P. A psychoneurotic reaction of delinquent boys and girls. *Journal of Abnormal and Social Psychology,* October, 1937, 32, 329-342.

Balser, Ben H. A behavior problem — runaways. *The Psychiatric Quarterly,* July, 1939, 13, 539-557.

Bard, Morton and Ellison, Katherine. Crisis intervention and investigation of forcible rape. *The Police Chief,* May, 1974, 41, 68-73.

Bayh, The Honorable Birch. Testimony at the Hearings of the House of Representatives Subcommittee on Equal Opportunities of the Committee on Education and Labor. Ninety-third Congress, second session. Reported in the proceedings of the above titled: *Juvenile Justice and Delinquency Prevention and Runaway Youth.* Washington,

D.C.: U.S. Government Printing Office, 1974, 159-164.

Bloom, Bernard L. Definitional aspects of the crisis concept. In Howard J. Parad (ed), *Crisis Intervention: Selected Readings.* New York: Family Services Association of America, 1965, 303-311

Bloom, Martin. *The Paradox of Helping: Introduction to the Philosophy of Scientific Practice.* New York: John Wiley and Sons, Inc., 1975.

Bobbit, O.P. (Director, Operation Peace on Mind). *Personal Correspondence.* October 3, 1977.

Bonee, John L. III. Runaway children. *Connecticut Bar Journal,* 1974, 48, 360-389.

Brecher, John. Wanted: 500 volunteers to help children just be their friends. *The Miami Herald,* October 2, 1975, Section B, 1-2.

Calhoun, Lawrence G., Selby, James W. and King, H. Elizabeth. *Dealing with Crisis.* Englewood Cliffs, N.J.: Prentice-Hall, Inc., 1976.

Caplan, Gerald. A public health approach to child psychiatry. *Mental Health,* 1951, 35, 235-249.

————. Preparation for the healthy parenthood. *Children,* 1954, 1(5), 171-175.

————. Patterns of parental response to the crisis of premature birth. *Psychiatry,* 1960, 23, 365-374.

————. *An Approach to Community Mental Health.* London: Tavistock Publications, 1961.

———— *Principles of Preventive Psychiatry.* New York: Basic Books, 1964.

Caplan, Gerald, Mason, Edward A., and Kaplan, David M. Four studies of crisis in parents of prematures. *Community Mental Health Journal.* Summer, 1965, 1, 149-161.

Christensen, Harold T. *Handbook of Marriage and the Family.* Chicago: Rand McNally and Co., 1964.,

Clarke, Eleanor. Round-the-clock emergency psychiatry services. In Howard J. Parad (ed), *Crisis Intervention: Selected Readings.* New York: Family Service Association of America, 1965, 261-273.

Clark, Ted and Jaffe, Dennis T. Change within youth crisis centers. *American Journal of Orthopsychiatry*, 1972, 42(2), 675-687.

Clarke, J. An analysis of crisis management by mental welfare officers. *British Journal of Social Work.* 1971, 1(1), 27-37.

Cobb, Charles. Runaway youth center opens doors. *The Florida Times-Union*, May 17, 1974, p.7.

Coelho, George V., Hamburg, David A., and Adams, John E. (eds). *Coping and Adaptation.* New York: Basic Books, 1974.

Cohen, Lawrence E. *Pre-adjudicatory Detention in Three Juvenile Courts: An Empirical Analysis of the Factors Related to Detention Decision Outcomes.* Albany, N.Y.: Criminal Justice Center, 1975.

Collins, Marilyn. *Personal Communication*, June 2, 1980.

Columbia Journal of Law and Social Problems. Nondelinquent children in New York: the need for alternatives to institutional treatment. 1972, 8, 251-265.

Conti, Anthony P. A follow-up investigation of families referred to outside agencies. *Journal of School Psychology*, 1973, 11(3), 215-223.

D'Angelo, Rocco. *Families of Sand: A Report Concerning the Flight of Adoloescents from Their Families.* Columbus, Ohio: School of Social Work, The Ohio State University, 1974.

Darbonne, Allen. Crisis: a review of theory, practice and research. *International Journal of Psychiatry*, 1968, 6(5), 371-379.

Decker, J.B. and Stubblebine, J.M. Crisis intervention and prevention of psychiatric disability: a follow-up study. *American Journal of Psychiatry.* 1972, 129(6), 725-729.

Duckworth, Grace L. A project in crisis intervention. *Social Casework*, 1967, 48(4), 227-231.

Dunford, Franklyn W. and Brennan, Tim. A taxonomy of runaway youth. *Social Service Review.* September, 1976, 457-470.

Easton, K.J. Volunteers critically needed to aid wayward juveniles. *Lake Worth Herald*, September 25, 1975, page 1.

El-Guebaly, Nady and Offord, David R. The offspring of alcoholics: a critical review. *The American Journal of Psychiatry*, 1977, 134(4), 357-365.

√English, Clifford J. Leaving home: a typology of runaways. *Transaction*, 1973, 10(5), 22-24.

Erikson, Erik H. *Childhood and Society*. New York: W.W. Norton and Co., 1950.

————. Growth and crisis of the healthy personality. In Clyde Kluckhorn and H. Murray (eds). *Personality in Nature, Society and Culture*. New York: Alfred Knopf, 1956, 185-225.

Finley, John. "Shelter house: for runaway youths, it's the light at the end of the tunnel," *Louisville Courier-Journal*, March 4, 1979

Gula, Martin. *Agency Operated Group Homes*. Washington, D.C.: U.S. Government Printing Office, Department of Health, Education and Welfare, Children's Bureau, 1964.

————. Community services and residential institutions for children. In Yitzhak Bakal (ed). *Closing Correctional Institutions*. Lexington, Mass: Lexington Books, 1973, 13-18.

Halpern, Howard A. The crisis scale: a factor analysis and revision. *Community Mental Health Journal*, 1975, 11(3), 295-319.

Hansell, Norris. *The Person-in-Distress: On the Biosocial Dynamics of Adaptation*. New York: Human Sciences Press, 1976.

Hart, James A. and Manella, Raymond L. The runaway youth act. *Juvenile Justice*, 1975, 26(4), 3-6.

Heilig, Sam M. Klugman, David J. The social worker in a suicide prevention center. In Howard J. Parad (ed). *Crisis Intervention: Selected Readings*. New York: Family Service Association of America, 1965, 274-283.

Helfer, Ray E. *A Self-instructional Program on Child Abuse and Neglect*. East Lansing, Mich.: Department of Human Development, Michigan State College of Human Medicine (no date indicated).

Henry, Kenneth (ed). *Social Problems: Institutional Inter-*

personal Perspectives. Glenview Illinois: Scott, Foresman, 1978.

Henvener, Phil. What kind of place is this? *The Houston Post,* February 9, 1975, pages 1 and 3a.

Hiatt, Catherine and Spurlock, Ruth E. Geographical flight and its relation to crisis theory. *American Journal of Orthopsychiatry,* 1970, 40(1), 53-57.

Hildebrand, James A. Why runaways leave home. *Journal of Criminal Law, Criminology and Police Science,* 1963, 54(2), 211-216.

Hill, Reuben. *Families under Stress.* New York: Harper and Bros., 1949.

Hill, Reuben. Generic features of families under stress. *Social Casework,* 1958, 39(2&3), 139-150.

_____. Social stresses on the family. In Marvin B. Sussman (ed). *Sourcebook in Marriage and the Family,* second edition. Boston: Houghton Mifflin Co., 1963, 303-314.

Hill, Reuben and Hansen, Donald H. The identification of conceptual frameworks utilized in family study. In Marvin B. Sussman (ed). *Sourcebook* in *Marriage and the Family,* second edition. Boston: Houghton Mifflin Co., 1963, 494-507.

Homer, Louise E. Community-based resource for runaway girls. *Social Casework,* 1973, 54(8), 473-479.

Horton, Paul B. and Hunt, Chester L. *Sociology,* fourth edition. New York: McGraw-Hill Book Co., 1976.

Howell, M.C., Emmons, E.B., and Frank, D.A. Reminiscences of runaway adolescents. *American Journal of Orthopsychiatry,* 1973, 43(5), 840-853.

Jacobson, Gerald F. Crisis theory and treatment strategy: some sociocultural and psychodynamic considerations. *Journal of Nervous and Mental Disease,* 1965, 141(2), 209-218.

Jenkins, Richard L. The runaway reaction. *American Journal of Psychiatry,* 1971, 128(2), 168-173.

_____. Deprivation of parental care as a contributor to juvenile delinquency. In Albert R. Roberts (ed). *Childhood Deprivation.* Springfield, Illinois: Charles C. Thomas, 1974, 116-135.

Jenkins, Richard L. and Boyer, Andrew. Types of delinquent behavior and background factors. *International Journal of Social Psychiatry*, 1967, 14(1), 65-76.

Jenkins, Richard L. and Glickman, Sylvia. Common syndromes in child psychiatry: deviant behavior traits. *The American Journal of Orthopsychiatry*, 1946, 16(2), 244-254.

Jenkins, Richard L. and Stahle, Galen. The runaway reaction: a case study. *Journal of the American Academy of Child Psychiatry*, 1972, 11(2), 294-313.

Johnson, Elmer H. *Social Problems of Urban Man*, Homewood, Illinois: Dorsey Press, 1973.

Joos, J., Debuyst, C. and Sepulchre-Cassiers, M. Boys who ran away from home: A Belgian study. *International Journal of Offender Therapy*, 1970, 14(2), 98-104.

Kaplan, David M. Observations on crisis theory and practice. *Social Casework*, 1968, 49(3), 151-155.

Kaplan, David M. and Mason, Edward A. Maternal reactions to premature birth. *The American Journal of Orthopsychiatry*, 1960, 30(3), 539-552.

Karp, H. Neil and Karls, James M. Combining crisis therapy and mental health consultation. *Archives of General Psychiatry*, 1966, 14(5), 536-542.

Kaufman, Joshua, Allen, James R. and West, Louis Jolyon. Runaways, hippies and marijuana. *American Journal of Psychiatry*, 1969, 126(5), 717-720.

Kehoe, Charles J. and Freer, Richard. Cooperative services for runaway youth. *Juvenile Justice*, 1977, 28(1), 35-39.

Keiffer, Elisabeth. Please. . . ask my mother if I can come home. *Good Housekeeping*, September, 1975, pages 85, 134 & 136.

Kerns, Elizabeth. Planned short-term treatment, a new service to adolescents. *Social Casework*, 1970, 51(6), 340-346.

Klaber, Jane K. Persons in need of supervision: is there a constitutional right to treatment? *Brooklyn Law Review*, Winter, 1973, 39, 624-657.

Koury, Michael Anthony. Crisis: identity. *Adolescence*, Summer, 1971, 6, 229-234.

Kritzer, H. and Pittman, F.S. Overnight psychiatric care in a general hospital emergency room. *Hospital and Community Psychiatry*, 1968, 19(10), 303-306.

Lachman, Sheldon J. *Psychosomatic Disorders: A Behaviorist Interpretation.* New York: John Wiley and Sons, 1972.

Langsley, Donald, Pittman, F.S., Machatka, P. and Flomenhoft, K. Family crisis therapy: results and implications. *Family Process*, 1968, 7(2), 145-158.

Langsley, Donald and Kaplan, David M. *The Treatment of Families in Crisis.* New York: Grune and Stratton, 1968.

Latina, Jane C. and Schembera, Jeffrey L. *Volunteer Homes for Status Offenders: An Alternative to Detention.* Tallahassee, Florida: Division of Youth Services, October, 1975, mimeographed.

Lester, Daniel and Brockopp, Gene W. (eds). *Crisis Intervention and Counseling by Telephone.* Springfield, Illinois: Charles C. Thomas, 1973.

Leventhal, Theodore. Control problems in runaway children. *Archives of General Psychiatry*, 1963, 9(2), 122-128.

————. Inner control deficiencies in runaway children. *Archives of General Psychiatry*, 1964, 11, 170-176.

Lindemann, Erich. Symptomatology and management of acute grief. *American Journal of Psychiatry*, 1944, 101(2), 141-148.

Looney, Lt. Pat. Commanding Officer, Juvenile Aid Bureau. Nassau County Police Department. *Personal Communication.* April, 1977.

Lovitt, Robert, Psychological consultation to a police training academy: problems and opportunities. *Community Mental Health Journal*, 1976, 12(3), 313-319.

Lowery, Lawson G. Runaways and nomads. *American Journal of Orthopsychiatry*, 1941,11(4), 775-783.

McQuade, Walter and Aikman, Ann. *Stress.* New York: E.P. Dutton and Co., 1974.

Margolin, Michael H. Styles of service for runaways. *Child Welfare*, 1976, 40(3), 205-215.

Martin, Christopher A. Status offenders and the juvenile justice system: where do they belong? *Juvenile Justice*, 1977, 28(1), 7-17.

Merton, Robert K. and Nisbet, Robert (eds). *Contemporary*

Social Problems. New York: Harcourt Brace Jovanovich, Inc., 1971.

Moos, Rudolf H. (ed). *Human Adaptation: Coping with Life Crises.* Lexington, Mass.: D.C. Heath and Co., 1976.

Morgan, Ted. Little ladies of the night. *The New York Times Magazine.* November 16, 1975, pp. 34-50.

Myers, Cynthia (Executive Director, National Runaway Switchboard). *Personal Correspondence.* November 17, 1977.

Mullin, Sue. How officials meet problems of runaways. *Washington (D.C.) Star,* February 5, 1979 pp. B5-6.

Nachmias, David and Nachmias, Chava. *Research Methods in the Social Sciences.* New York: St. Martin's Press, 1976.

National Council on Crime and Delinquency. Board of Directors. Jurisdiction over status offenses should be removed from the juvenile court: a policy statement. *Crime and Delinquency,* 1975, 21(2), 97-99.

National Runaway Switchboard. *First Year Report.* Chicago: Metro-Help, Inc., 1975. mimeographed.

————— *Annual Report 75-76.* Chicago: Metro-Help, Inc., 1976. mineographed.

Neugebauer, William. Kids run away from woes. *Daily News (New York),* February 11, 1979, Brooklyn Section, pp.1 and 3.

New York State Council of Voluntary Child Care Agencies. Ad Hoc Committee on the Court Related Child. *Report on PINS and Related Issues.* February 25, 1975, mimeographed.

New York Times. Texan said to admit role in 25 killings. August 10, 1973, pages 1 & 44.

—————. Too many persons missing each year to rouse suspicion. August 11, 1973, page 17.

—————. Police in Houston explain procedure on runaways. August 14, 1973, page 18.

—————. Midwest teenagers tell of forced vice. November 15, 1977, page 29.

New York University Law Review. Runaways: a non-judicial approach. April, 1974, 49, 110-130.

Opinion Research Corporation. *National Statistical Survey on Runaway Youth, Part I.* Final report on a study conducted for the Office of Youth Development, Department of Health, Education and Welfare. Princeton: Opinion Research Corporation, June, 1976.

_____. *National Statistical Survey on Runaway Youth, Part II.* Final report on a study conducted for the Office of Youth Development, Department of Health, Education and Welfare. Princeton: Opinion Research Corporation, November, 1976.

Outland, George E. The federal transient program for boys in southern California. *Social Forces,* 1936, 14(3), 427-432.

_____. Determinants involved in boy transiency. *Journal of Educational Sociology,* 1938, 11(6), 360-372.

Parad, Howard J. and Caplan, Gerald. A framework for studying families in crisis. *Social Work,* 1960, 5(3), 3-15.

Parad, Howard J. (ed). *Crisis Intervention: Selected Readings.* New York: Family Service Association of America, 1965.

Parad, Howard J. and Parad, Libbie, A study of crisis-oriented short-term treatment. *Social Casework,* 1968, 49 (6&7), 346-355 and 418-426.

Parad, Howard J. Crisis intervention. In Robert Morris (ed). *Encyclopedia of Social Work.* Volume I. New York, National Association of Social Workers, 1971, 196-202.

Pasewark, Richard A. and Albers, Dale A. Crisis intervention: theory in search of a program. *Social Work,* 1972, 17(2), 70-77.

Paul, Louis. Crisis intervention. *Mental Hygiene,* 1966a, 50(1), 141-145.

_____. Treatment techniques in a walk-in clinic. *Hospital and Community Psychiatry,* 1966b, 17(2), 49-51

Paulsen, James A. Runaway girls from suburbia. *American Journal of Orthopsychiatry,* 1967, 37(2), 402-403.

Pawlak, Edward J. *The Administration of Juvenile Justice.* University of Michigan, Ph.D. dissertation, 1972.

Paykel, Eugene S., Myers, Jerome K., Dienelt, Marcia N., Klerman, Gerald L., Lindenthal, Jacob J., and Pepper, Max P. Life events and depression: a controlled study. *Archives of General Psychiatry.* 1969, 21(6), 753-760.

Polsky, Howard W. Vision and process: the quality of life in community group homes. In Yitzhak Bakal (ed). *Closing Correctional Institutions: New Strategies for Youth Services.* Lexington, Mass.: Lexington Books, 1973, 59-66.

Poplin, Dennis E. *Social Problems.* Glenview, Illinois: Scott, Foresman, 1978.

Porter, Robert A. Crisis intervention and social work models. *Community Mental Health Journal*, 1966, 2(1), 13-21.

Raab, Selwyn. Pimps establish link to the midwest. *New York Times*, October 30, 1977, pages 1, 21.

————. City plans new strategy to deal with prostitutes under age of sixteen. *New York Times*, November 2, 1977, page B3.

Raphling, D.L. and Lion, J. Patients with repeated admissions to a psychiatric emergency service. *Community Mental Health Journal*, 1970, 6(4), 313-318.

Rapoport, Lydia. The state of crisis: some theoretical considerations. *Social Service Review*, 1962a, 36(2), 211-217.

————. Working with families in crisis: an exploration in preventive intervention. *Social Work*, 1962b, 7(3), 48-56.

————. Crisis-oriented short-term casework. *Social Service Review*, 1967, 41(1), 31-42.

————. Crisis intervention as a mode of brief treatment. In Robert W. Roberts and Robert H. Nee (eds). *Theories of Social Casework.* Chicago: University of Chicago Press, 1970, 267-311.

Rector, Milton G. PINS cases: an American scandal. *Social Issues Resources Series*, November, 1974, 1, 1-6.

————. Juvenile justice issues and priorities. Paper read at the First Anniversary Luncheon, New York State Council of Voluntary Child Care Agencies, May 9, 1975.

Reinherz, Helen and Griffin, Carol Lee. The treadmill of failure: early school failure and later academic and vocational aspirations and achievement in Henry Wechsler, Helen Reinherz and Donald Dobbin. *Social Work Research in the Human Services.* New York: Human Sciences Press, 1976, 208-235.

Rhine, M.W. and Mayerson. P. Crisis hospitalization within a psychiatric emergency service. *American Journal of Psychiatry*, 1971, 127(10), 1386-1391.

Riemer, Morris D. Runaway children. *American Journal of Orthopsychiatry*, July, 1940, 10, 522-526.

Ritter, Father Bruce, The Adolescent Runaway: A National Problem. *U.S.A. Today*, March, 1976, 24-28.

Roberts, Albert R. Suicide and suicide prevention: an overview. *Public Health Reviews*, 1973, 2(1), 3-30.

_____. (ed). *Childhood Deprivation*. Springfield, Ill.: Charles C. Thomas, 1974.

_____. Police social workers: a history. *Social Work*, 1976, 21(4), 294-299.

Robey, Ames, Rosenwald, Richard J., Snell, John E. and Lee, Rita E. The runaway girl: a reaction to family stress. *American Journal of Orthopsychiatry*, 1964, 34(4), 762-767.

Robins, Lee N. and O'Neal, Patricia. The adult prognosis for runaway children. *American Journal of Orthopsychiatry*, 1959, 29(4), 752-761.

Rode, Alex. Perception of parental behavior among alienated adolescents. *Adolescence*, 1971, 6(21), 19-38.

Rosenheim, Frederick C. Techniques of therapy. *American Journal of Orthopsychiatry*, July, 1940, 10, 651-659.

Rosenwald, R. J. and Mayer, J. Runaways girls from suburbia. *American Journal of Orthopsychiatry*, 1967, 37(2), 402-403.

Sarri, Rosemary C. *Under Lock and Key: Juveniles in Jails and Detention*. Ann Arbor, Michigan: National Assessment of Juvenile Corrections, Universtiy of Michigan, December, 1974, mimeographed.

Selye, Hans. *The Stress of Life* New York: McGraw-Hill, 1956.

Shaw, Clifford R. *The Jack-roller*. Chicago: University of Chicago Press, 1930.

Sheehy, Gail. *Passages: Predictable Crises of Adult Life*. New York: E.P. Dutton and Co., 1976.

Sheilds, L. Family crisis intervention. *Journal of Psychiatric Nursing and Mental Health Services*, 1969, 7(5), 222-225.

Shellow, Robert, Schamp, Juliana R., Leibow, Elliot and

Unger, Elizabeth. *Suburban Runaways of the 1960's*. Monographs of the Society for Research in Child Development. 1967, 32(3), 1-51.

Sheppard, Nathaniel Jr. With 20,000 runaways in city, police are confident that chances for a mass tragedy are slight. *New York Times,* August 16, 1973, page 17.

Sifneos, Peter E. A concept of "emotional" crisis. *Mental Hygiene*, April, 1960, 44, 169-179.

Spector, Gerald A. and Claiborn, William L. (eds). *Crisis Intervention*. New York: Behavioral Publications, 1973.

Sterba, James P. Texas police find four more bodies: the total is now 23. *New York Times*, August 14, 1973, pages 1 & 17.

————. Texas toll of boys rises to 27 in nation's biggest slaying case. *New York Times*, August 14, 1973, pages 1 & 18.

Stewart, Elbert W. *The Troubled Land: Social Problems in Modern America*. New York: McGraw-Hill, 1972.

Stierlin, Helm. A family perspective on adolescent runaways. *Archives of General Psychiatry*, 1973, 29(1), 56-62.

Stiller, Stuart and Elder, Carol. PINS — a concept in need of supervision. *The American Criminal Law Review*, 1974, 12, 33-60.

Strickler, Martin and Allgeyer, Jean. The crisis group: a new application of crisis theory. *Social Work*, 1967, 12(3), 28-32.

Suddick, David E. Runaways: a review of the literature. *Juvenile Justice*, 1973, 24(2), 47-54.

Sussman, Marvin (ed). *Sourcebook in Marriage and the Family*. Boston: Houghton Mifflin Co., second edition, 1963; third edition, 1968.

Taplin, Julian R. Crisis theory: critique and reformulation. *Community Mental Health Journal*, 1971, 7(1), 13-23.

Time Magazine, August 27, 1973, page 57.

Troll, Lillian E., Neugarten, Bernice L. and Kraines, Ruth J. Similarities in values and other personality characteristics in college students and their parents. *Merrill-Palmer Quarterly*, 1969, 15(4), 323-336.

United States Department of Health, Education and Welfare. Intra-Departmental Committee on Runaway Youth. *Run-*

away Youth: A Status Report and Summary of Projects. Washington, D.C.: Department of Health, Education and Welfare, March 31, 1976, mimeographed.

United States House of Representatives. Hearings of the Subcommittee on Equal Opportunities of the Committee on Education and Labor. *Juvenile Justice and Delinquency Prevention and Runaway Youth.* Ninety-third Congress, second session. Washington, D.C.: U.S. Government Printing Office, 1974.

United States Senate. Hearings before the Subcommittee to Investigate Juvenile Delinquency of the Committee on the Judiciary. *The Runaway Youth Act.* Washington D.C.: U.S. Government Printing Office, January 13, 1972.

Vecsey, George. For young urban nomads, home is the streets. *New York Times,* June 1. 1976, pages 37 & 59.

Vinter, Robert D., Downs, George and Hall, John. *Juvenile Corrections in the States: Residential Programs and Deinstitutionalization.* Ann Arbor, Michigan: National Assessment of Juvenile Corrections, University of Michigan, 1976, mineographed.

Walfish, Steven, Tulkin, Steven R., Tapp, Jack T. and Russell, Mary. Criteria for appropriate and inappropriate referrals to a crisis clinic. *Community Mental Health Journal,* 1976, 12(1), 89-94.

Wein, Bibi. *The Runaway Generation.* New York: David McKay Co., 1970.

Weisman, Steven R. Cities setup efforts to aid runaway children. *New York Times,* September 3, 1973, page 8.

Woodward, Kay. *Personal Communication.* Governor's Office for Volunteer Services, Austin, Texas, June 24, 1980. p. 1.

Youth Reporter. Newslink. September, 1974, page 2.

Zastrow, Charles and Navarre, Ralph. Help for runaways and their parents. *Social Casework,* 1975, 56(2), 74-78.